Drive and Stroll in the

Cotswolds

Richard Shurey

First published 2005
© Richard Shurey, 2005

COUNTRYSIDE BOOKS
3 Catherine Road
Newbury, Berkshire

To view our complete range of books,
please visit us at
www.countrysidebooks.co.uk

ISBN 1 85306 894 2

Photographs and maps by the author
Cover picture of the Upper Coln Valley supplied by Bill Meadows

Designed by Peter Davies, Nautilus Design
Produced through MRM Associates Ltd., Reading
Printed by Woolnough Bookbinding Ltd., Irthlingborough

Contents

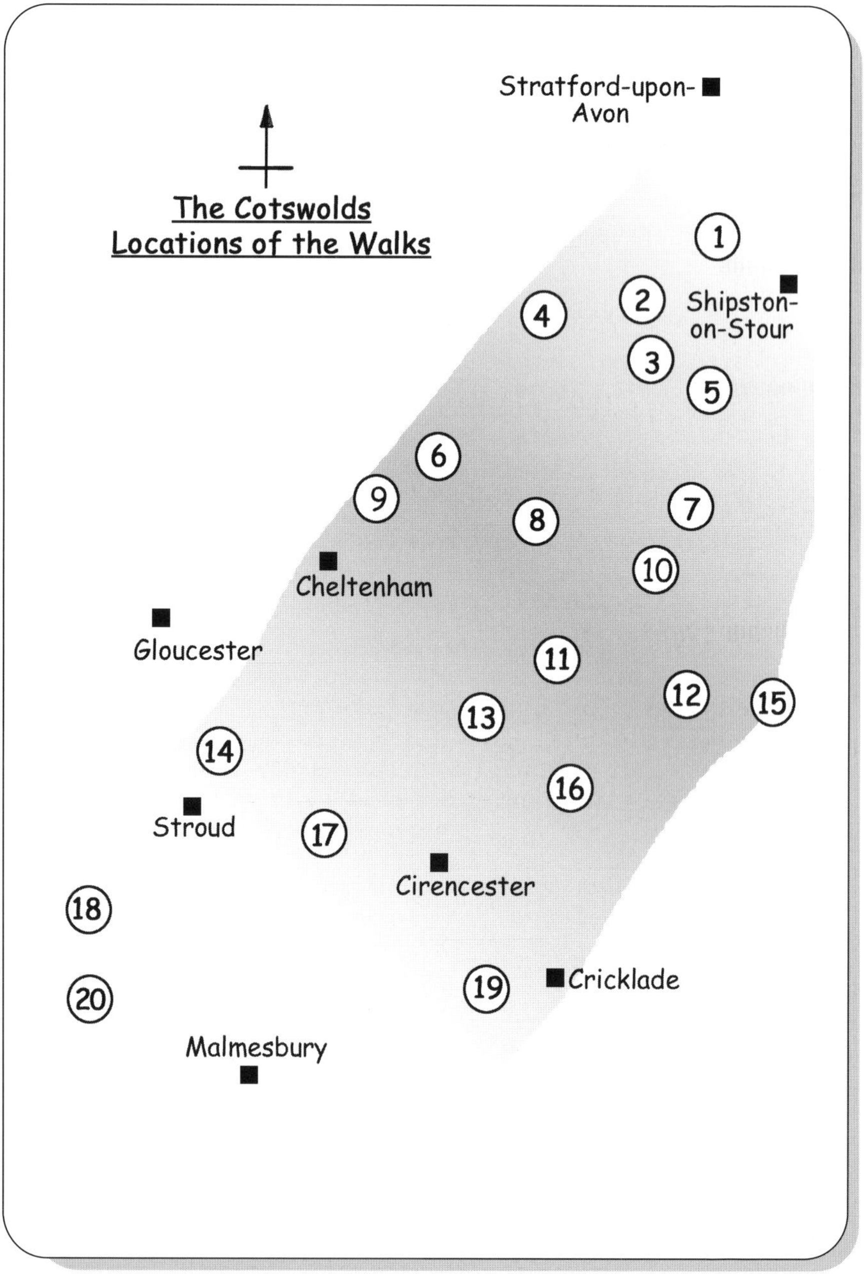

The Cotswolds
Locations of the Walks

Stratford-upon-Avon ■

① 1

② 2   Shipston-on-Stour ■

④ 4

③ 3

⑤ 5

⑥ 6

⑨ 9

⑧ 8

⑦ 7

⑩ 10

Cheltenham ■

Gloucester ■

⑪ 11

⑫ 12   ⑮ 15

⑬ 13

⑭ 14

⑯ 16

Stroud ■

⑰ 17

Cirencester ■

⑱ 18

⑳ 20

⑲ 19   ■ Cricklade

Malmesbury ■

Contents ❦

Publisher's Note

We hope that you obtain considerable enjoyment from this book; great care has been taken in its preparation. Although at the time of publication all routes followed public rights of way or permitted paths, diversion orders can be made and permissions withdrawn.

We cannot, of course, be held responsible for such diversion orders and any inaccuracies in the text which result from these or any other changes to the routes nor any damage which might result from walkers trespassing on private property. We are anxious though that all details concerning the walks are kept up to date and would therefore welcome information from readers which would be relevant to future editions.

The simple sketch maps that accompany the walks in this book are based on notes made by the author whilst checking out the routes on the ground. However, for the benefit of a proper map, we do recommend that you purchase the relevant Ordnance Survey sheet covering your walk in particular, the Explorer OL45 (The Cotswolds) covers most of the area of these walks and is large scale. The Ordnance Survey maps are widely available, especially through booksellers and local newsagents.

Introduction

What is your idea of a 'heaven on earth?' Mine is the view on a sunny day in springtime coming over the hill from Ilmington and into the blossom-speckled valley in which Chipping Campden nestles. The horizon is the wooded ridge where Broadway Tower glints in the sunshine . . . and I know more treasured glories are hidden beyond. Those lovely places are in my beloved Cotswolds, which many years ago was designated as an AONB – an Area of Outstanding Natural Beauty.

I will not follow some and call them the Cotswold Hills. This is a misnomer. It is a limestone mass with a high scarp edge running from Chipping Campden in the north to Bath in the south. Behind this scarp the plateau dips gradually eastwards but it is cut into by valleys containing little brooks that encouraged communities to settle. Now these are villages of exquisite beauty that (of local weathered stone) seem not to be man-made but natural features of the countryside.

But why Cotswolds? It was about 1,500 years ago that a farmer called Cod tilled the rocky soil near Winchcombe. His upland farm was known as Cod's Wold. Gradually the name encompassed more and more of the Wolds to embrace the area we know today.

The purpose of this book is to encourage you to share with me the glory of the Cotswolds. We have to use the car as a necessity to reach the area as public transport is not extensive enough but, once in the region, the only way to get into the heart of the country and sample the beauty is to forsake four wheels for two feet. These are only short walks but long enough to marvel at the wonders of the English countryside at its best, then to rest at some of the most attractive welcoming pubs.

The area once supported a solely agricultural economy with sheep rearing of a distinctive breed called Cotswold Lion creating great wealth. Several of the small towns have beautiful 'wool' churches built with generous gifts from wool merchants and we visit several on the walks.

Sheep rearing has given way to arable farming in many areas. At first it was thought that the soils were not rich enough with the stony fields but the experiments in the Second World War discovered that, with good husbandry, excellent crops of barley could be harvested.

The many footpaths used in the walks are invariably well-maintained. For this we are greatly indebted to the voluntary Cotswold Wardens who ensure that routes are waymarked and obstacles removed. Then there is the Cotswold Way which we use here and there on some of the rambles – a hundred-mile route from Chipping Campden to Bath. It is now a splendid National Trail and you may be tempted to tackle the whole Way after sampling it!

The Cotswolds are surely a place that unfortunate expats in far-off lands wistfully sigh for – and we are lucky enough to be able to visit and enjoy the delights. Happy strolling!

Richard Shurey

1 Ilmington

On the hills above Ilmington

The Walk 5½ miles
Map OS 1:50,000 Landranger 151 Stratford-upon-Avon. GR 210440

How to get there

Take the A3400 out of Stratford-upon-Avon. Within 4 miles turn right. The lane is signed to Ilmington which is reached after 3½ miles. Just after the Ilmington sign keep ahead along the road signed to Mickleton. After 300 yards the playing field car park is on the left.

Drive and Stroll

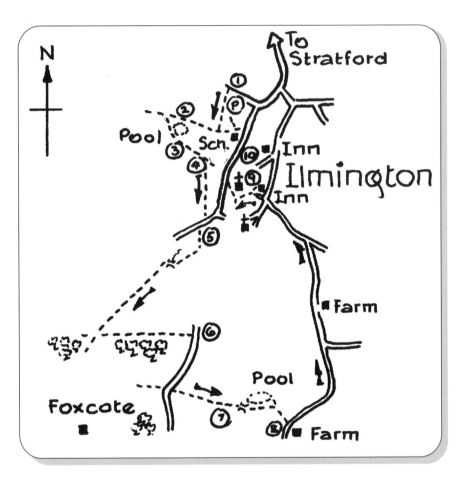

Introduction

We tend to think of the Cotswolds as Gloucestershire lands. But surrounding counties such as Warwickshire nudge into Cotswold territory with the distinctive buildings and scenery that evolve from the limestone strata.

Ilmington (from 'the elm-grown hill') where the walk starts is a lovely village from which hills rise to the highest point in Warwickshire at 850 ft. There are a few houses of brick; my theory is that these were considered rather special – stone for buildings was merely dug out of the ground from local quarries on the hillsides; brick had to be manufactured elsewhere.

There are several interesting features in the village to see including (overlooking the Lower Green) the stocks. These are only a replica of the originals which are in the museum at Mary Arden's House near Stratford-upon-Avon. Near the Upper Green is the village pound where stray animals were kept. Also near here is Crab Mill House (that was the home of one of the few women Nobel prize winners – Professor Hodgkin) and the old school which is now the Catholic church.

From the car park on the playing field you can see the Pavilion which dates from the 1930s and the sports area which had the first lottery grant in the Midlands. The route then goes through pastures before starting to climb the high hills. The views are now wide and beautiful, far over the Avon Vale.

A lane on the outskirts of the village is crossed then there is a steep climb. Away to the left are the 'humpty-dumpty' fields which were once quarries. The path leads to a ridge overlooking the grand mansion of Foxcote.

Descending, a peaceful mere cupped between hills is passed – man-made with surrounding dipping willows. Quiet lanes return the walker to the village.

Refreshments

There are two pubs in Ilmington. The Red Lion is more workaday where good but standard 'with chips' fare is available with an especially tasty ploughman's. Telephone 01608 682366. The Howard Arms is more upmarket. The menu changes frequently but can include 'different' soups and seasonal dishes such as game. Telephone 01608 682226.

THE WALK

Out of the car park turn left along the road. About 200 yards past the speed derestriction sign climb a stile on the left. In the pasture follow the arrowed direction to bear left to pass a stile that may be isolated and obsolete. Climb the stile in the far corner. Walk a few steps by a left hand hedge to another stile. Do not climb it but turn 90 degrees right. Walk down the middle of the next two fields. Nearing the far end climb a stile on the right.

At once turn left to climb another stile.

Walk uphill to a stile where two paths are signed. Over the stile, take the left hand way to go downhill.

The hedge on the left is one of many hereabouts that has recently been replanted. Strangely it was funded by government grants as only a decade or so previously farmers were paid to remove hedges to increase food production.

We overlook a small pool. This was where, in the 17th century, many 'took to the waters' for health reasons.

At one time it was thought that the medicinal properties could make Ilmington a spa. The well house was

Ilmington post office

demolished in 1860 but a stone from the well was recently found and is displayed on the Upper Green.

Go through the trees to the right of the pool then climb the rise to a stile by an electricity supply post. Take the arrowed direction over the ridge and furrow field (that indicates old 'strip' farming) to a stile in the far right diagonal corner.

Two paths are signed. Take the path over the stile. Walk along a path by a left hand hedge. There are now good views over the village. Drop down to a corner stile and keep ahead (still by a left hand hedge). Climb a double stile near the corner. Walk down steps to a road. Cross and turn right.

Within a few yards climb a stone stile left. Walk between gardens to a meeting of paths. Turn right along a fenced path. Climb a stile to a rough pasture and go over a bridge. Keep ahead to a bridge on the right which is high above a brook. Turn left in the field. Follow the borders of hill pastures to the top of the ridge.

The large house in the valley is Foxcote. This Palladian-style mansion with large columns dates from the 18th century, and was the home of the Howard family. It is now owned by a rich American who has created many 'instant' woods to improve the shooting.

Turn left along a bold track to a lane. Turn right. Outside the gates of Foxcote climb a stile on the left and walk downhill.

On the distant horizon you can see the domed Brailes Hill. This is capped by a clump of beech trees and is the second highest hill in Warwickshire. Even further is a sharp end of Edge Hill. Here was the first battle of the Civil War in 1642.

Follow a way to the very far right hand corner. Climb the stile and walk along the clear path through the trees. Go over a little rivulet and keep the pool on the left. Pass through a metal gate to a farm tractor way. Turn right to a lane.

Turn left. Keep ahead at a junction. At a T-junction turn left to a cross roads in Ilmington. Go over to Ballards Lane to the left of the Red Lion. The lane becomes a tarmac path to a T-junction of paths. Turn left to pass at the rear (and by the garden) of Ilmington Manor.

The Manor is a fine Elizabethan house and was once owned by the De Montfort family. Interestingly it was from the Manor that the first Christmas broadcast by George V in 1934 was introduced by Walton Handy, the village shepherd. The Traditional Ilmington Morris Dancers perform in the garden during the summer months.

Follow the tarmac path to Ilmington church and the lane. Turn right so the church is on the right.

St Mary's church has fine Norman arches. Children love to hunt the church mice – there are eleven carved on the furnishings. The woodwork was installed in the 1930s by Thompson of York – a mouse is their trademark.

Walk along the lane past the school (built about 25 years ago) and go through a kissing gate on the left. Follow the fenced path a few steps then go through a gate right. A clear path goes over the fields to a gate to the playing field.

Places of Interest Nearby

Stratford-upon-Avon – and the Shakespeare houses – are 8 miles away. On a hill to the west are the National Trust gardens of Hidcote which were created nearly a hundred years ago by the American Lawrence Johnston.

2 | Chipping Campden

The (now dry) Cart Wash

The Walk 3 miles
Map OS 1:50,000 Landranger 151 Stratford-upon-Avon. GR 154395

How to get there

Take the A3400 out of Stratford then turn right (signed Broadway) along the B4632. At Mickleton bear left: the B4081 leads to the church at Chipping Campden. Parking is available at Campden School near the church or in the road near the church.

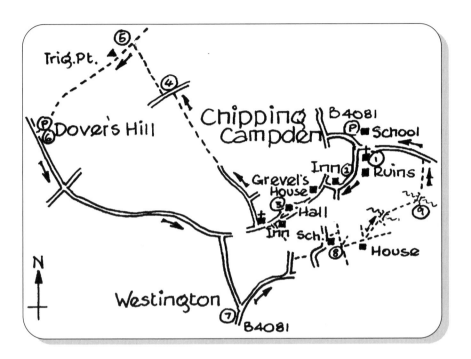

Introduction

Chipping Campden's High Street was described by the historian G.M. Trevelyan as 'The most beautiful village street left in the island'. It is a delicious amalgam of building styles of many centuries, all in that warm stone – there is only one building with a brick facing!

Many of the buildings are of standard width which was the width of the medieval burgage plots; the layout can be clearly seen from aerial photographs.

We walk down the main street which was planned a hundred years after the Domesday Survey by Hugh de Gondeville – a favourite courtier of Henry II. We pass fine homes that were built by the 14th-century rich merchants such as William Grevel. (He was described on a brass in the church as 'the flower of the wool merchants of all England'.)

Opposite the Volunteer Inn our walk now follows the route of the Cotswold Way, a 100-mile long-distance path that runs from Chipping Campden to Bath. Hoo Lane becomes a bridleway and there is a steep climb to the breezy ridgetop above the town then onto the National Trust lands of Dover's Hill.

Drive and Stroll

Besides the splendid views, the hill supports an important habitat for wildlife. The rougher scrubland slopes are loved by many songbirds such as chaffinch, whitethroat and yellowhammers.

There is a lane off the ridge, then (now on the outskirts of Chipping Campden) we walk through the hamlet of Westington where there are wonderful examples of the thatcher's art.

After a road section there are footpaths over river pastures. We have views of the ruins of Campden House. The great house was built by William Hicks, a great benefactor of the town in the 17th century. His home only lasted forty years before it was set on fire during the Civil War. The walk ends at the beautiful 'wool church' of St James'.

Refreshments

There are many pubs and tea rooms in the town catering for all tastes and pockets. Near the start is the 14th-century Eight Bells – the oldest inn in the town. Try their steak pie and those wicked chips – after the walk, of course! Telephone 01386 840371.

THE WALK

The walk starts at the church of St James.

The 'wool church' was largely rebuilt in the 15th century with the wealth from wool. The place derives from the little 12th-century Norman church. The building contains many treasures including the 14th-century priest's cope. The tower (1500) is 120 ft high. During the age of wool, fleeces came from all parts of the kingdom and passed through Chipping Campden for export to the Low Countries.

Walking away from the church along Church Street pass the elaborate

gateway to Campden House and the almshouses given to the town by the great benefactor Sir Baptist Hicks. Continue by the Eight Bells Inn to the High Street. Turn left. Wool merchant William Greval's house is on the other side of the road. A little plaque on a house on the left tells us that here lived C.R. Ashbee. Cross to the opposite side of the High Street. Turn left.

C.R. Ashbee was a social reformer who created the Guild of Handicrafts in London's East End to counter the low quality mass-produced goods. He saw many empty properties in run-down Chipping Campden and the Guild migrated en masse to the town in 1902. Ashbee ran education classes, re-formed the Morris Dance

At the top of Dover's Hill

group and restored houses and factory buildings. Sadly people at the time wanted cheap rather than crafted goods and the Guild folded after only six years. Many workers stayed – Harts the silversmiths in Sheep Street is a fascinating place to visit.

 ③

Walk past the Market Hall (another gift of Baptist Hicks) and the lively and popular Baptist church. Near the end of the High Street and by the Catholic church turn right along Hoo Lane. Keep ahead past a junction and when the lane ends to go along a footpath, climb to the road at the top of the ridge.

 ④

Cross and turn left for 150 yards. Turn right along a well-worn fenced track. Away to the right is Ilmington Hill (at 850 ft the highest hill in Warwickshire) and the lower flat-topped Meon Hill which is capped by an Iron Age fort. Go through a kissing gate to the National Trust lands of Dover's Hill.

Dover's Hill is named after the flamboyant Robert Dover. In 1612 he transformed a small Whitsuntide feast into a grand festival of sport and pageantry which he called the Cotswold Olimpicks. The games were stopped in 1852 because of

15

Drive and Stroll

rowdyism. They were revived a few decades ago for the Friday after the Spring Bank Holiday.

Turn left and pass the triangulation plinth. Continue to the toposcope.

The toposcope is dedicated to Frederick Landseer Gibbs. Aided by G.M. Trevelyan he bought Dover's Hill, in about 1926, for £4,000 to save it from a hotel development. In 1929 it was presented to the National Trust.

Go through the car park to a lane. Turn left and keep ahead at a crossroads. Drop down the hill to a road junction on the outskirts of Chipping Campden. Take the lane right to the B4081 at Westington.

Turn left. Past beautiful thatched roofed cottages, the road twists sharp left at a road junction. Within 200 yards take a path right (sign on concrete post). Join an estate road and keep ahead. Within 150 yards (as the road bends sharp left) keep ahead along a path with a school on the right. Through a metal barrier we come to a tarmac path.

Turn right for a few steps. Two paths are signed on the left. Take the right-hand path to walk along a house drive. Pass the house and stables. The path divides; take the left-hand path. Cross the brook. Bear right. Away to the left is an isolated gateway, tall stone buildings and some ruins. This was Campden House.

Campden House was a splendid house built by Sir Baptist Hicks between 1613 and 1619 at a cost of £44,000. In 1645, during the Civil War, it was burnt down by retreating Royalist troops.

Follow the path through a kissing gate and across a stream. Bear left over the pasture and continue to a road. Turn left to the church and the car park.

Places of Interest Nearby

Hidcote Gardens (National Trust) are wonderful. They were set out by the American Lawrence Johnston on a high inhospitable site. There is a good restaurant for a cream tea but check on opening times on 01684 855370. The voluntary Cotswold Wardens lead guided tours of **Chipping Campden** for groups of any size upwards of twelve people. The tour lasts about three hours including a preliminary audio-visual show and a cream tea at the end. For details phone 01386 832131.

3 | Blockley

Blockley, the capital of all stone villages

The Walk 4 miles
Map OS 1:50,000 Landranger 151 Stratford-upon-Avon. GR 164350

How to get there

Take the A44 Evesham to Moreton-in-Marsh road, then signed lanes to
Blockley. There is streetside parking alongside the wall opposite the post
office near the church.

17

Drive and Stroll

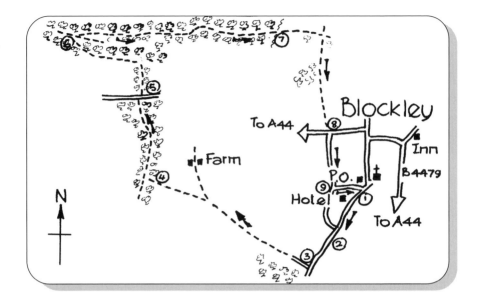

Introduction

Blockley has been called 'the capital of all stone villages' with so much stone crammed into such a small area. It spreads up either side of a valley from a brook. The brook played an important part in Blockley's industrial past right from the Domesday Survey of 1086, when twelve mills were listed, to a century or so ago when this was the centre of silk manufacture.

The strong waters tumbling off the hills powered many silk mills where the raw material was made for the ribbon industry of Coventry. The mill owners built fine houses for themselves and rows of cottages for the workers – both types of buildings are sought after today.

The only sad thing I find about the beautiful town is the loss of many small shops that once lined the main street. Now converted into rather elegant houses, we can visualise the past with the plethora of old shop fronts and the names given to the dwellings. Overlooking all is the fine 18th-century tower of the church.

The walk starts along the main street then climbs out of the valley beside rich arable fields which were once vast sheep runs. Over a lane we plunge into fine woodlands of mixed trees where game birds scatter as the walker approaches.

There are good tracks which emerge from the woods by a gentle stream. A steep climb leads back to a hill above Blockley. There are fieldpaths (now on the long distance path of 'the Heart of England Way') then lanes lead back to the little town that is now so peaceful, but which was once a hive of industry.

Refreshments

There are now two inns in Blockley – in recent times there were six! The Great Western Arms is the more workaday with a good range of basic fare – especially recommended are the baguettes and home-made soups. Telephone 01386 700362. The Crown is for that something special and the chef also offers to prepare your own favourite dish. Try the twice-baked goats cheese souffle! Telephone 01386 700245.

THE WALK

①

Walk along Bell Lane with the post office on your right and the church away to the left.

The church belonged to the Bishops of Worcester a thousand years ago. There are many stones that were put in place by the Normans. The bishops had their palace where the Manor House now stands. There are many monuments to the Rushouts who lived at the great house of Northwick a mile or so away.

②

Follow the way along the High Street passing the Crown Inn to reach a lovely spot and a name plaque.

There is continuous gushing water from a wall on the right – the Russell Spring. 'Water from the Loving Rock – God's precious gift to man' we are reminded. There was a scheme a few years ago to bottle this water to help lower the rates – *the plan was abandoned! On a gatepost is a plaque to tell us that Joanna Southcott lived here from 1804 to 1814. She was a prophetess and the Joanna Southcott Society is still active.*

③

At a road junction near the end of the High Street turn right along Day's Lane. At the end go through a gate to arable lands. Keep ahead at the border of the field. About 300 yards before silos on a farm the path bears left over an open field. Out of the field keep the same direction a few steps through a wood to a wide track.

④

Turn right. Follow the track to a lane. Turn right. Within 200 yards take a signed path through a gate on the left.

⑤

Walk along a wide track. The track soon turns 90° left to keep near the border of the wood with fields on the left. Keep along the clear way which bears right to drop down the valley to a meeting of ways.

Turn right. Do not walk along the track which hugs the valley but the path marked by a small green arrow on a post that bears left climbing out of the valley.

Note the hollows which mark the old quarries. In this area before you built a house you dug a hole to get some stone!

The path is near the edge of the woods with fields on the left. Keep along the track to pass through a gate to leave the woods.

In a pasture bear right to climb the steep hill and pass through large trees on the ridgetop. Bear right over a rough pasture. Pick up a right hand wire fence and follow it to a corner stile. Keep the direction over a crossing path and through a hedge gap to an arable field. Follow the well-used path to houses and a lane.

Cross to another lane. This leads to a little green.

This is called Back Ends. This was once a lively spot as it was the site of the traditional fairground.

Turn left at the junction. On the way back to Blockley we pass a little building on the right.

This is a little village hall (one of two in Blockley). It was once a chapel and was built in 1794. It is now partly used as a doctor's surgery.

Places of Interest Nearby

Two and a half miles along the lane north of Blockley is **Broad Campden**. Here is a little 18th-century Quaker Meeting Room. On the way you may get a glimpse of **Northwick Park**. Now separate apartments, it was the seat of the Rushout family.

4 Broadway

Broadway Tower was built in 1800

The Walk 4 miles
Map OS 1:50,000 Landranger 150 Worcester, The Malverns and surrounding area. GR 100377

How to get there

From the north, drive along the A44 from Evesham. At a roundabout nearing Broadway take the road signed to the village. There is a car park (fee paying) off the B4632 Stratford Road.

Drive and Stroll

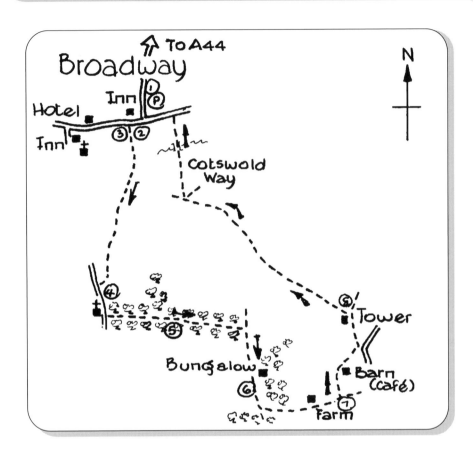

Introduction

The walk starts from Broadway which suffers from being known as the prettiest village in the Cotswolds. The traffic has been greatly reduced since a by-pass was built a few years ago but still the crowds come to mask the beauty in summertime. The answer therefore is to visit this delightful place out of season.

The walk starts over lowland meadows; the way is clear and indicated by a series of kissing gates – the route here has been made a stile-free pathway by the Cotswold Wardens.

Following a visit to the rather isolated St Eadburga's church there is a steady climb along a sometimes muddy track called Coneygree Lane. This was the way to the upland village of Snowshill until a new road was built up the valley a century ago.

Out of the trees and into hill pastures we have magnificent views with the highest point of the Cotswolds (Cleeve Hill, 1,083 ft above sea level) on a distant horizon.

The high path continues by woodlands to Broadway Country Park. This is privately owned and incorporates a deer park, picnic areas and children's playground. Dominating the area is Broadway Tower. The top can be climbed in the summer months – it is said that 13 counties can be seen from the lofty viewpoint.

Out of the Country Park we pass through a kissing gate to join the long-distance route of the Cotswold Way. There are some fine new stiles which have been built with Government funding after the Way became a National Trail.

The fine views now are far over the Avon Vale with the sinuous river twisting its way to the Severn. We pass through rough pastures that were once quarries where stone was hewed to construct Broadway's lovely buildings. The route is now well-waymarked to a street at Broadway.

Refreshments

There were once 30 inns at Broadway. Only a handful remain. The Horse and Hounds is near the car park and serves a wonderful snack that would please any hungry ploughman. Telephone 01386 852287.

THE WALK

 ①

From the car park walk to the main road and turn left to a mini-roundabout on the High Street. Cross and turn right.

Broadway (Bradnwege in Anglo-Saxon times) was on the great route from Wales to London. From about 1600 the importance of the place increased with the growth of stage coach travel. Many inns sprang up for serving the travellers and for changing horses before climbing up the steep Fish Hill to the top of the escarpment.

 ②

Walk along the High Street and under a clock.

The clock was erected to commemorate the Golden Jubilee of Queen Victoria in 1887. It was renovated by public subscription in 1953 (coronation of Queen Elizabeth II) and again to mark the golden wedding anniversary of the Queen and Prince Philip.

 ③

A few steps further take a path signed 'To Swings and Things'. Follow the walled way to a recreation

The celebrated Lygon Arms, Broadway

ground and a meeting of paths. Keep ahead beside a right hand fence to a corner kissing gate. Follow a route marked by further kissing gates to a lane. Turn left to pass a converted gatehouse called The Court.

This place was the entrance to the stables of Broadway Court which stood in the meadow opposite until its demolition in 1773. The gate-house was derelict until its 'rescue' in 1898.

④

Keep along the road to the ancient church dedicated to St Eadburga.

St Eadburga's church was the parish church of Broadway until 1840 when a new place of worship was erected in Broadway. The ancient church is an amalgam of Norman and Gothic styles. There is a simple Norman font and look for the tall mounting block by the entrance.

⑤

Take the signed path opposite the church. This climbs to a T-junction of paths. Turn right. Go over a stile by a gate to a rough hill pasture. Bear left and aim to the right of a bungalow.

Climb a stile by the bungalow. Bear left along a cart track. Just before a wood take the signed path left over a stile by a gate. Keep ahead to go by a junction of cart tracks and pass a farm and barns.

Opposite a plantation of young trees take a path over a stile left. Walk over the grass to a kissing gate by a field gate. Go to the left of a barn (a restaurant in summertime). Continue to the park entrance. Just before the entrance go through a tall kissing gate. Follow the way heading towards Broadway Tower.

A small monument is passed. This tells us that a Whitley bomber on a training flight crashed here in June 1943 killing the five members of the crew.

Broadway Tower was constructed in 1800 by the Duke of Coventry on an old beacon signal site. The family seat was at Croome Court near Pershore. It was a folly said to have been used to signal to the Countess that her husband was on his way home.

Go through the kissing gate to the right of the tower. Turn left and climb a stile. Now descending from the ridge follow the waymarked Cotswold Way to a road at Broadway. Turn left to the mini-roundabout where we were before. Retrace your steps to the car park.

Places of Interest Nearby

Snowshill Manor is three miles along a lane south of Broadway. In this manor house there is an extraordinary collection of bric-a-brac assembled by the rather eccentric Charles Paget Wade. It is open from about April to October but check before the visit (01386 852410). The village of Snowshill was used for the film of *Bridget Jones's Diary*.

5 | Moreton-in-Marsh

Redesdale Hall

The Walk 4 miles
Map OS 1:50,000 Landranger 151 Stratford-upon-Avon, Warwick and Banbury. GR 205327

How to get there

The starting place of Moreton-in-Marsh is on the A425 from Warwick to Cirencester. There is a car park (fee paying) near the station or park on a quiet side street.

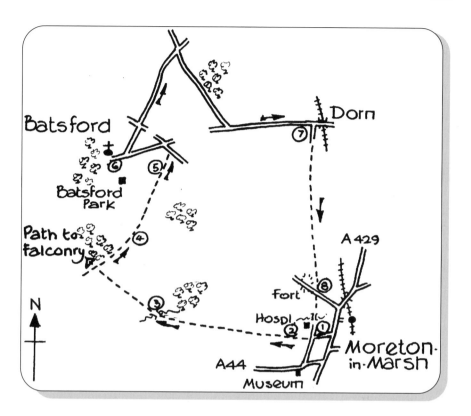

Introduction

The origin of the name of Moreton-in-Marsh (not 'in the') is a little obscure. Certainly the settlement was on a drier gravel area and surrounded by damp lowlands but Moreton was once Moreton Henmersche. 'Mersche' was related to 'marc' signifying a march or boundary. The counties of Warwickshire, Worcestershire, Gloucestershire and Oxfordshire meet near here.

It is a town of stone buildings with the axis being the main wide street which still accommodates a weekly market each Tuesday. Unfortunately this street is also the Roman's Fosse Way and the busy A429.

Much of the old wealth was founded on wool but this trade disappeared in Stuart times. There was also a linen industry in the 18th century. It was in the next century that the manorial rights were purchased by Baron Redesdale. The Redesdales' seat was at Batsford Park and we start the walk in the main street at Redesdale Hall which was a gift from Lord Redesdale.

Drive and Stroll

The first mile or so is over lowland pastures then borders the parkland of Batsford. We have fine views of the great mansion across the deer park. This was the home where the celebrated Mitford girls grew up. You may spot an eagle – there is a falconry at Batsford. A lane leads to the village which is little more than a few estate houses and a church.

We are now at an important watershed of England as some waters from streams go westwards to the Bristol Channel and others to the North Sea.

Quiet lanes lead to the hamlet of Dorn then a pathway goes over sheeplands to a road. Nearby are the earthworks of a Roman fort with the Fosse Way now a short distance away. A path through a small town park crosses a brook then we return to the High Street.

Refreshments

Many inns and tearooms can be found in Moreton-in-Marsh. The Swan Inn at the corner of Bourton Road and High Street is open all day. It sells Flowers Ales and also offers bed and breakfast. Telephone 01608 650711.

THE WALK

① From Redesdale Hall in the High Street, go along nearby Corders Lane.

Near the Hall is the ancient two-storey Curfew Tower with a bell that is never rung. The medieval building has been used for a lock-up and has a 17th-century clock.

 ②

At the end of Corders Lane cross to the opposite signed footpath. Go along allotments and pass through a kissing gate to a meadow. Keep the heading with more gates to show the way. We are now on the long-distance path called the Monarch's Way.

The Monarch's Way follows the extensive journeys of Charles II. He is said to have stayed at Moreton's White Hart Inn in July 1644.

 ③

Go over a stone bridge. The waters of this stream flow into the Thames. Keep ahead through more gates. At a stone wall on the right turn right through a gate.

 ④

Follow the path with the deer park of Batsford on the left.

Batsford House looks Elizabethan but only dates from Victorian times. The beautiful Mitford girls lived here. All had exciting lives. Unity and Diana were great admirers of Hitler. The last sister is the Duchess of

Devonshire who lives at Chatsworth. See Burford walk (page 71).

Keep ahead to a lane. Turn left then left again at a junction.

This lane leads to Batsford village. The church here was built by Frances Mitford in 1860 in the Norman style. There are inevitably many monuments to the Redesdales.

Turn right at the church to a crossroads. Go straight over then right at the next crossroads and left at a T-junction. This way leads to the hamlet of Dorn.

At the start of the hamlet take a signed path on the right. Walk down a wide track then keep ahead through sheep pastures. Go through a kissing gate to enter the last field before the road. Bear left to go onto the road.

Note the grassy mounds to the right. This is the site of the Roman fort. The Roman road through Moreton was raised two feet to reduce the gradients of the bridges when the railway came in 1848.

Cross to the recreation ground. Walk to the far side to cross a bridge to a road. Turn right to Moreton.

Places of Interest Nearby

Outside Moreton on the Oxford Road was a large RAF station for training aircrew. It is now a famous training centre for firemen but many mementoes of the RAF days are gathered in the **Wellington Museum** which is open daily. It is in the centre of Moreton on the A44 Evesham Road. (01608 650323)

Four miles south-east (just off the A44) is **Chastleton House**. This is a National Trust property said to be 'one of England's finest and most complete Jacobean houses' which dates from 1612. The policy of the Trust has been to conserve it rather than restore it to a pristine state. Opening days and times vary from March to November so telephone first (01608 674355).

6 Winchcombe

Sudeley Castle

The Walk 4 miles
Map OS 1:50,000 Landranger 151 Stratford-upon-Avon, Warwick and Banbury. GR 205327

How to get there

Winchcombe is on the B4632, 7 miles north-east of Cheltenham. There is a signed car park (fee paying) off the High Street or park on the street by the church.

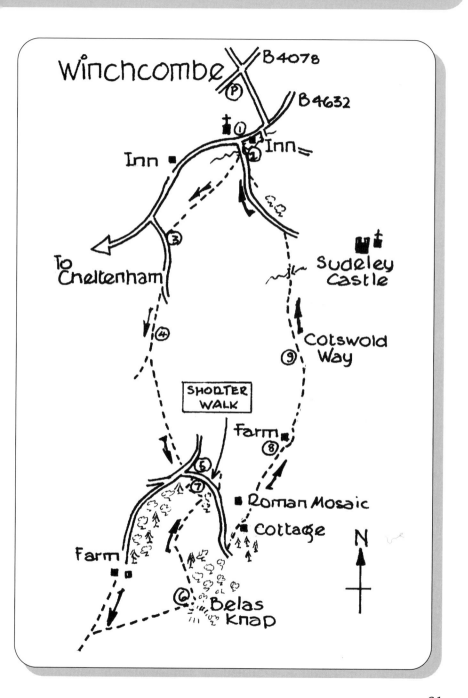

Drive and Stroll

Introduction

The little town of Winchcombe is cupped in a fold of the high hills – 'a windy place' some say. It was once the capital of the region of the Saxon kingdom called Winchcombshire.

King Kenulf founded a great abbey here in 798 on the site of a nunnery built by King Offa a hundred years earlier. Pilgrims journeyed from afar both to Winchcombe and to the Cistercian Hailes Abbey a mile or so away. Nothing remains of Winchcombe Abbey which closed in 1540 although it is thought many stones were used in the Perpendicular church (whose tower overlooks the town) and in citizens' houses in Cowl Lane and the High Street.

Weaving was an important industry for 500 years until it declined in the 17th century. Some of the local mills switched to the manufacture of paper.

The walk starts from the main street and down Vineyard Street opposite the church. There are some very ugly gargoyles on the church! Vineyard Street used to be called Duck Street after the ducking stool which was situated by the river. Over the little Isbourne the route is across fields to a lane. From here there is a steady climb with fine views over the town and across to the distant Cleeve Common – the highest point of the Cotswolds at over 1,000 feet above sea level.

At the top lane there is a choice of ways. The shorter way misses out the well-preserved long barrow of Belas Knap. After a wood delightfully called Humblebee we start descending from the ridge.

Nearby (hidden in a wood) is the site of a Roman house then we go past the elegant house of Wadfield. Further down the hill there are fine views of Sudeley Castle. Over pastures and arable fields (which can be rather 'gooey' in wintertime!) a lane is joined. This goes past the entrance gates of Sudeley Castle then back to Winchcombe.

Refreshments

There are many inns and cafés in Winchcombe. The Plaisterers' Arms in the old Market Square is popular with walkers. The baguettes are well filled and the soups are good for a winter's day. Telephone 0124 2602358.

THE WALK

From the High Street walk down Vineyard Street. Cross over the River Isbourne.

The Isbourne is unusual in that (unlike most streams and brooks) it is said to run 'against the sun' which some say is unlucky.

Just over the bridge go through a kissing gate on the right. Walk at the side of the pasture and pass (not go through) a kissing gate. Bear half left over the field to pass through a kissing gate in the corner. Follow the clear path at the borders of fields to a gate to a lane.

Turn left. Within a third of a mile take a signed path through the entrance gates of Corndean Hall.

Glance a few yards ahead and you will see a wartime pillbox. These are becoming rare in the countryside but were once a common site. They were manned by 'Dad's Army' and sited in strategic places to stem the advance of an invading army.

Follow the vehicle drive. As this bears right, climb a stile to the hill pasture on the left. Regain the old heading now climbing the hill. Pass an isolated waymark post. About 150 yards before a billowing oak tree the path bears off slightly to the left to pass another waymark post which may be rather concealed by a fallen tree. Continue climbing to a stone stile to a lane by a junction.

For the shorter walk take the lane ahead. For the full route turn right on the lane. When the lane divides take the left fork which is signed Hill Barn. Go past a farmstead; the lane has now become a rough cart track. Within 500 yards take a signed footpath left.

At the end of a long track climb a stone stile to Belas Knap.

This long barrow was built about 2500 BC and was used for successive burials over several centuries. For some unexplained reason there is a false portal. When excavated, remains of 35 humans were found – also animal bones and pottery.

Climb the stile out of the complex and turn left to walk beside a wood then at the edge of a large sheep pasture. Go through a gate and stay at the edges of fields along a clear path to a metal kissing gate by a metal field gate into woods. The track drops down steeply to a lane.

Turn right. Pass one signed path on the left. At the next (signed Cotswold

Drive and Stroll

Way) turn left down a wide track to pass Humblebee Cottages. Keep on the rough track.

In the pine wood on the left is a small hut which is usually unlocked. The hut was erected there to protect a fine section of mosaic pavement inside, and which was once inside a Roman house.

The Cotswold Way is a 100-mile long distance footpath that runs from Chipping Campden to Bath. It has recently been made into a National Trail so will receive additional Government funding.

We reach a farmstead. Keep the farm and the fine house called Wadfield on the left. Walk along a fenced way. We now have our first view of Sudeley Castle.

The castle dates mainly from the 15th century. It was badly damaged in the Civil War. In 1479 the place was given to Sir Thomas Seymour who married Henry VIII's widow Catherine Parr. She was buried in the 15th-century church after dying in childbirth.

At the end of the fenced way climb a stile. Take the arrowed direction to walk at the side of the field. In a far corner turn left to stay at the side of the field to a step stile and plank bridge.

Walk at the border of an arable field and go over a bridge across a brook. Walk over the open field to a stile by a white marker disc. Keep ahead in a constant direction over the fields to emerge on a lane. Turn left to Winchcombe.

Places of Interest Nearby

To the north of Winchcombe a steam railway runs. It is the GWR – the **Gloucestershire and Warwickshire Railway**. There are fine steam engines and the Father Christmas 'special'. Telephone 01242 621405 for times of trains. A few miles south-west of Winchcombe is the pleasant town of **Cheltenham**. There are elegant shops, floral displays and Regency terraces.

7 Stow-on-the-Wold

Deep in the Cotswold countryside at Upper Swell

The Walk 4 miles
Map OS 1:50,000 Landranger 163 Cheltenham and Cirencester Area.
GR 195256

How to get there

Stow-on-the-Wold lies on the Fosse Way (A429) at the junction with the A436, B4068, A424, B4077. (It is said that 'all roads in Gloucestershire lead to Stow'!) There is a car park (fee paying) off the A436 on the south of the town.

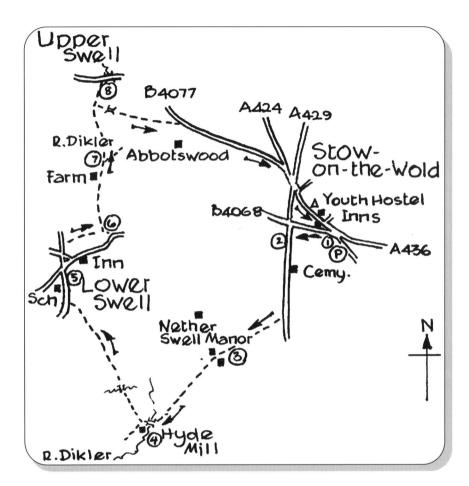

Introduction

'Stow-on-the-Wold-where-the-wind-blows-cold' runs the saying. At 800 ft above sea level (the highest town in the Cotswolds) it is the coldest place in the wolds; indeed it holds records for the coldest in all England. Usually towns are situated in sheltered valleys where there is abundant water but Stow is different and water shortages have been a problem over the centuries with bore holes having to be dug deep for an adequate supply.

With many highways meeting here this has always been a place catering for travellers, with posting houses and inns, blacksmiths and ostlers.

This was also a wealthy wool town with sheep grazing on the slopes of the ridge. We read that Daniel Defoe reported 20,000 sheep being sold here at one fair. Although cars have sadly taken over the market square there are still notable horse fairs in the town when travelling folk come from all parts of the country.

After a perambulation of the town there is a walk beside the busy A429. This is the Roman's highway – the Fosse Way. The route is now on the Gloucestershire Way – a long-distance path that meanders through the county. It goes through woods that cling to the steep hillside then descends to a large equestrian centre by the 'modern' Nether Swell Manor which dates from 1909. Across sheep meadows we come to the River Dikler. Here there is the splendid Hyde Mill.

There is now a lonely stretch of lowland above the river – this is another long-distance route – the Heart of England Way which runs from Cannock Chase in distant Staffordshire to end at Bourton-on-the-Water.

We reach one of the Cotswold 'gems' – Lower Swell which has an interesting church that is a mixture of the old and the new. The walk continues along the valley of the Dikler which has been dammed here and there to form delightful pools on the way to Upper Swell.

We rejoin the Gloucestershire Way for a road section alongside a magnificent example of Cotswold stone walling. This runs beside the estate of Abbotswood all the way back to Stow on its high hill.

Refreshments

There are many eating and drinking places in Stow. At Lower Swell is the Golden Ball Inn – a typical country inn that specialises in home-made food but try the 'Traditional Sunday Roast' – it really is as good as mother's! Telephone 01451 830247.

THE WALK

①

Out of the car park turn left along the A436. Just before the traffic lights the parish church is on the right.

St Edward the Confessor church had an original foundation in AD 870 but it was in the 15th century that the wool merchants used some of their great wealth to build the tall, massive tower. A mile to the north is the site of the last significant skirmish of the Civil War in 1646 when 1,000 Royalist prisoners were held for some days in the church.

②

Turn left along the A429. Within half a mile cross and take a signed footpath along a farm track which soon borders a wood. At the end go through a hunting gate. In the field

Drive and Stroll

follow the arrowed way to a gate to a wood. Follow the clear track to a gate to a field. Follow a fence on the left to descend the hills. Pass through several gates to a farmstead, part of Nether Swell Manor.

We are now walking along the Monarch's Way. This long-distance pathway traces the tortuous route King Charles II took through Worcester to the coast at Shoreham.

Keep ahead to pass a house with a balcony. Look for a signed path on the left clearly marked off the vehicle way. Resume the old heading then rejoin the vehicle way so by-passing a house. Continue ahead to go through a fence gap by a huge barn. Walk along an embankment then drop down steps to a gate. In a pasture go along a well-used path to a far gate.

Look back over the field. Here are the ridges and furrows of medieval strip farming. The strips were usually about 200 yards long and 15 yards wide; the troughs were once drainage ditches or footpaths between strips.

Go through a gate by the attractive Hyde Mill. Pass through two small white gates then cross the water. Past a cottage go through a metal gate then another. We are now on the Heart of England Way. Walk along a fine grassy path heading to the right-hand side of a wood. Cross a wide bridge over a brook and pass through a metal gate. Bear left along a wide farm track. Keep ahead to pass large cattle barns. Walk along a vehicle way to a road at Lower Swell.

Many records say Swell does not have connections with the little river but rather the word derives from the Old English 'swell', used as a hill or ridge. Another derivation, however, says the word is from Old English 'swelgan' – a spring. We do indeed read that the place may have been made into a spa in 1807 when medicinal waters were discovered. The little church has work of the Normans and there is a splendid series of animal carvings.

Turn right to a road junction. Go left then immediately right along a lane signed to Upper Swell. Within 200 yards take a path signed on the right along a vehicle way. At the end pass through a little gate. Walk by a stone wall on the right then bear right over the open pasture. Nearing houses swing left to a step stile onto a house drive.

Turn left. This is the drive to Abbotswood where there is a fine park with trees and lakes.

Abbotswood is a lovely mansion designed by Sir Edward Lutyens. For some years it was the home of Harry Ferguson, the farm tractor millionaire.

Beyond some houses and a dovehouse (which I thought was very old but is dated 1917!) go through a metal kissing gate on the left so leaving the drive. Take the arrowed direction. Follow a wire fence on the left to a far corner kissing gate. Continue ahead along a fenced way then pass through another kissing gate then another. Next is a squeeze stile to a pasture. Cross to another squeeze stile. Continue ahead to a road at Upper Swell.

This is a pretty village although on quite a busy road. There is an ancient bridge over the Dikler with a mill beyond. By the road is the Tudor Manor House (1600) and a church with much work from the 12th century.

Retrace your steps to pass through the two squeeze stiles. At once through the second turn left along a fenced way to cross the river. Go over a stile and climb the hill alongside a right hand wall then a wire fence to a stile to the B4077. Turn right. On the way back to Stow pass a water trough dated 1883 fed by a spring and admire the very long Cotswold stone wall (no mortar used!). There is a path alongside the road.

Places of Interest Nearby

A little over a mile to the north-west of Stow-on-the-Wold is the little **Donnington Brewery**. Although not open to the public its setting by the lakes and River Dikler is charming and well worth seeing. Two miles north of the town is **Banks Fee**, the home of Longborough Fesitval Opera. The performances are over several weeks during June and July. Telephone 01451 830292.

8 Guiting Power

The old cross at Guiting Power

The Walk 2½ miles
Map OS 1:50,000 Landranger 163 Cheltenham and Circencester Area.
GR 096246

How to get there

From Stow-on-the-Wold take the B4068 towards Cheltenham. After 5 miles Guiting Power is signed along a lane to the right. There is a car park near the church (donation towards parking welcome!)

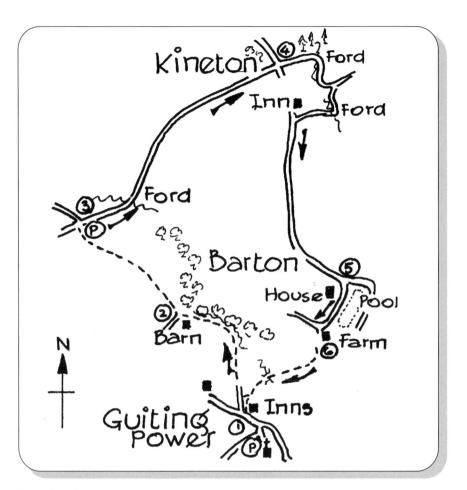

Introduction

How times change! Towards the end of the 19th century many houses were empty in Guiting Power. The reason? Depression in the agricultural industry – especially falling wheat prices. Today the lovely village is much sought after with wonderfully restored cottages that no doubt were once humble farm workers' dwellings.

The church, too, that was ruinous during the times of poverty had its chancel rebuilt half a century or so ago but much of the work of the Norman builders remains.

Strangely the name Guiting comes from the Old English 'gyte' which means 'flood'. Guiting Power is perched on slopes well above the little willow-fringed River Windrush and certainly not in danger from flooding. There are vast bare uplands where the wind can blow hard but modern farming methods ensure that good crops are harvested.

There are two village greens in Guiting Power (or Lower Guiting as it was once called). Here there is a delicious mixture of stone cottages and an inn and shop. We first have a path that soon borders the little river which meanders through woodlands. A farm track goes over lonely countryside and along a lane that crosses a ford – an idyllic place this. We then climb to the little hamlet of Kineton. The charm here lies with the two fords that enabled the farm tracks to cross the river.

Along a winding lane in the valley we reach another tiny hamlet – Barton. There is finally a fieldpath that climbs out of the vale to Guiting Power with its welcoming inns.

On the village green are two plaques in memory of members of the Cochrane family. One is to Ellis Raymond Cochrane who was Lord of the Manor for 40 years until his death in 1998. He was said to have been the 'kindest benefactor'. Sally Cochrane's memorial says that she gave much to the village and was 'enchantingly beloved'.

Refreshments

There are two inns in Guiting Power. Both are good. The Farmer's Arms is on the village green and the Hollow Bottom is just out of the village. The former is more workaday with standard pub fare. Telephone 01451 850358. The Hollow Bottom is open all day and is renowed for its sporting connections – especially horse racing. There are very rare meals here for the adventurous! How about ostrich steak or kangeroo fillet? Telephone 01451 850392.

THE WALK

From the village green walk along the road with the post office on your right. Within a few steps take a lane on the right signed as a no-through-road and the Wardens' Way.

The Wardens' Way was created by the volunteer Cotswold Wardens as a beautiful waymarked walk along the twenty or so miles from Winchcombe to Bourton-on-the-Water.

The lane becomes a rough vehicle track then a yellow limestone path. The path twists a way through woods with the infant River Windrush on the right.

The lovely-sounding name Windrush may be derived from the far-off Welsh with their 'gwym' meaning 'white'. The second part may be the Celtic 'reisko' fen or moor.

②

Climb the hill to a barn at the end of a lane. Do not walk along the lane but turn right along a farm road.

③

At a junction with a rough lane (a little car park is here) turn right. The lane drops down to a ford. Cross the water over the footbridge and climb out of the valley. The lane then drops down to Kineton.

④

At a crossroads take the opposite lane which descends to the two fords. Note the clapper bridges.

The clapper bridge is one of the oldest forms of bridges. The earliest date from prehistoric times. They all used flat stones of whatever material that was locally available.

Climb back to the road at Kineton and turn left. Follow the road to Barton.

There is a large mansion here that dates from the 18th century. It overlooks a pool (fed by the Windrush) that once provided the powering water for Barton Mill.

⑤

As the road swings sharp left keep ahead along a vehicle track to pass the pool on the left. Follow the way around bends and past a farmstead. On a bend look for a footpath sign pointing ahead along a farm drive. Pass Little Windrush Farmhouse then go to the left of a garage with blue doors.

⑥

Climb a stile and keep the direction to a second in a corner then climb another. Bear right over an open pasture to pick up a right hand fence to climb a stile tucked in a corner. At once go left to cross the water. Go up the rise by a left hand wire fence. Cross a cart track and go over the stile ahead. This way leads back to Guiting Power.

Places of Interest Nearby

Within five miles north-west of Guiting Power is **Hailes Abbey**. Founded by the Cistercians in 1246, the ruins really are spectacular where one can marvel at the skill of the masons. The National Trust site is managed by English Heritage. Telephone 0117 975 0700.

Opposite the Abbey is **Hailes church**. It stands in a field and includes the work of the Normans. The walls are decorated by medieval paintings.

9 Cleeve Hill

The clubhouse provides excellent refreshments

The Walk 4 miles
Map OS 1:50,000 163 Cheltenham and Circencester Area. GR 989272

How to get there

From Cheltenham, go along the B4632. Within 4 miles and at the top of Cleeve Hill take a right turn at a crossroads. The lane is signed to a golf course. Go over a cattle grid by the clubhouse and at once turn left to the free car park in an old quarry.

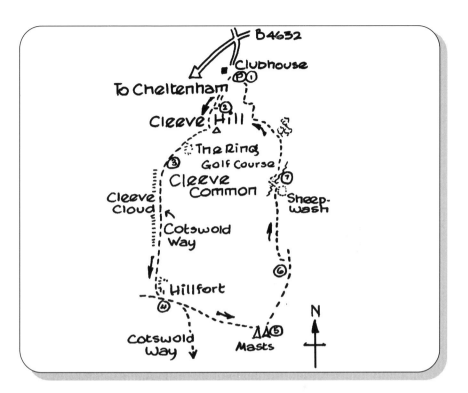

Introduction

Cleeve Common can be a wild place especially if the wind is blowing. It is the last unenclosed land in the high wolds and contains the highest points of the Cotswolds with one place almost 1,100 ft above sea level. Parts have the character of open moorland and one should take care if there is mist. Often there are few landmarks and walkers have been lost on these uplands. But it is also an exhilarating place with wonderful views – in fact a 'good to be alive place'!

The walk starts at the car park that is in a worked-out quarry. Over many centuries limestone has been extracted from Cleeve Hill. Now the man-made undulations add to the grandeur. There are many archaeological features: early on we pass a circular enclosure with a ditch and bank called The Ring. There is some uncertainty as to its purpose – but it might have been a ritual circle before stones were set in place.

A steep climb leads to a trig point – not the highest summit of the Common but more attractive than the real loftiest upland a mile or so to the south.

The walk then borders Cleeve Cloud – a magnificent cliff that marks the eastern border of Cleeve Common. This was a very strategic position to the warriors of old so it is not surprising that a large hill fort was constructed. It covers over two acres and includes a double rampart.

We pass near a large stone called Huddlestone's Table. Sir John Huddlestone was granted manorial common rights on Cleeve in the 16th century but it was also the spot where the King of Mercia, Kenelm, gave a speech after the dedication of Winchcombe Abbey.

A gentle climb leads to the landmark radio masts. These are in fact the last good landmarks for the next mile as we walk over a flat grassland moor before picking up the waymarks of the Cotswold Way back to the car park.

Refreshments

There is an excellent restaurant in the golf clubhouse which is open to the public. The food and choice is excellent and the prices are the most modest I found on my 'strolls'. Try the beef and Stilton pie – just right for a hungry walker. Vegetarians enthused about the cauliflower cheese. The hours of opening vary so it is best to check before a visit. Telephone 01242 672025.

THE WALK

①

Climb to the black and white waymark post seen from the car park. Walking directly away from the car park, take the arrowed direction with the clubhouse to the right. Following the waymark posts cross one wide track to another. Turn left following the indicated direction. Climb the hill along a bold stony track.

②

By a quarry (with seats) the track bears sharp right. We are reassured (as there are many tracks) by the sight of another black and white post. Here bear left, climbing up the hill along a wide grassy path. At the next post (Cotswold Way) take the path left. Meg, my dog, soon tired of chasing rabbits – there were so many! Gain the summit of the hill.

③

Turn right. Keep on a constant heading over hollows and hummocks to reach the scarp edge. Turn left to walk above the cliff called Cleeve Cloud.

The name comes from the Old English 'clef' – a cliff, and the Old English 'clud' – a rock.

Turn left and keep along the top of the escarpment following the waymarker posts to the ditches and banks of an Iron Age hillfort.

④

Keep along the scarp edge to a path going left. We are now heading towards three tall masts. When the Cotswold Way goes to the right through a gate, keep heading towards the masts and pick up the side of a wall. Continue for about 200 yards beyond the masts.

At a gate and notice board take the path signed left. Take care now. The path is not marked on the ground and we are on a vast flat grass moor. Take the direction indicated by the sign then head towards the right hand side of the chequered far distant Nottingham Hill. Keep a constant heading to pick up a right hand wire fence then continue to meet another black and white waymarker. This indicates we are again on the Cotswold Way.

Turn left. The route bears left dropping towards a deep gulley (where there are old terraced quarry workings) and away from a wire fence. A stony track goes down to a pool.

The pool feeds the stone sheepwash just a few yards away. Sheepwashes were an important part of the shepherd's life. The animals are subject to a number of skin parasites and to destroy them they are put through disinfectant.

Cross the little brook and turn right along a clear path. We go by a wood then start the steep climb. Keep eyes peeled for the black and white waymark posts as there are many other paths crossing the track back to the car park.

Places of Interest Nearby

Cheltenham is only a few miles away. This is one of the finest spa towns of Europe with elegant shops and beautiful formal gardens and it is said that 'here you can forget the cares of the world'. Two hundred and fifty years ago Cheltenham was a little stone village. Then in 1715, a mineral spring was discovered and by 1738 the first pump room was in place.

10 Bourton-on-the-Water

The mill at Lower Slaughter

The Walk 5 miles
Map OS 1:50,000 Landranger 163 Cheltenham and Cirencester Area.
GR 170210

How to get there

Bourton-on-the-Water is just off the A429, 14 miles north-east of Cirencester. There are two (fee paying) car parks in Bourton. One is by the signed 'Birdland' and the other in Station Road.

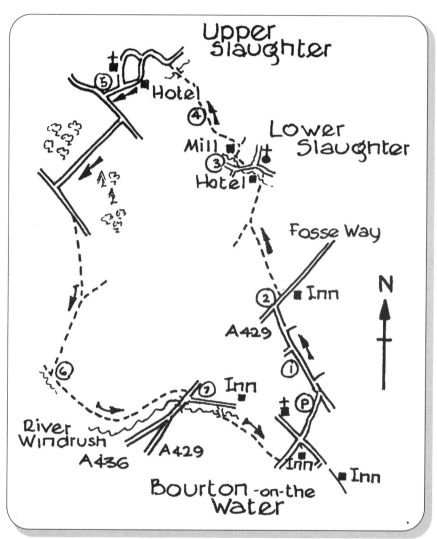

Introduction

One of my old guide books writes so succinctly about Bourton-on-the-Water – 'everything looks so calm that we become calm too'. My only caveat to this would be to add . . . 'away from the summer season'. Come in the summer and the beauty could well be masked by the influx of visitors.

The large village is unashamedly pretty and builds its tourist trade on it. Here the placid River Windrush flows beside the main street and many little stone bridges span the clear water where ducks glide with the slow current.

The 'attractions' are there to please visitors of all ages. We find a fascinating model village at the rear of an inn; 'Birdland' makes good use of the water with a collection of exotic birds; I love the excellent model railway layout and nearby is the motor museum. Add the rather up-market shops and eating places and there is more than enough to keep you in Bourton! However, this walk shows the Cotswolds at their beautiful best so do not be dissuaded!

Station Road leads to the Roman's highway of the Fosse Way which is now the busy A429. We then have a flat path (which has been upgraded by Cotswold Wardens to make it ideal for disabled walkers). Over the idyllic waterway of the River Eye we reach the gem of Lower Slaughter.

The lane nudges the river then passes a scene that artists love – there is an old water mill complete with its wheel and tall chimney alongside cottages of mellowed stone.

The path across the water meadows to Upper Slaughter is called the Wardens' Way. (The route runs along the valleys of little rivers to Winchcombe.)

Upper Slaughter has that 'away from it all' remoteness with little corners showing attractive cottages, a manor house, a Norman church, a little ford – and few people!

The route along lanes climbs over the ridge where the views are wide and beautiful. We drop down to the valley of the Windrush to rejoin the Wardens' Way to take us back to Bourton.

Refreshments

Bourton has many excellent inns, restaurants and cafés. A particular favourite of mine is The Old Manse Hotel overlooking the river. (The place started life in 1748 as the house of the local Baptist minister.) Their sandwiches are imaginative and well filled although I am always tempted by the roast meals here! Telephone 01451 820082.

THE WALK

From either car park the walk starts along Station Road to the A429.

The station (and its railway) have long gone but it was a most attractive route crossing the 700 ft contour from Banbury to Andoversford where it joined with the Andover line (the last main line to be built in the county in 1881). The line served many very remote communities and it is interesting to see how isolated were many of the stations.

Bourton-on-the-Water

At the traffic lights cross the main road and turn right. Within a few hundred yards take a signed path through a gate on the left. Keep ahead to cross the River Eye to a road at Lower Slaughter. Turn left.

Slaughter comes from the Old English 'slohtre' and means a place of pools or a muddy place. There is a Manor House with a dovecote in the garden. The church is modest and was mostly rebuilt in 1867.

Follow the left hand river then at a bridge cross and stay by the water

to the mill. At the far side go left along the Wardens' Way.

Watermills were known to the Greeks and are thought to have been brought to England by the Romans. At the Domesday Survey (1086) 5,264 watermills were recorded in the country.

Gates and waymark arrows show the way to a lane at Upper Slaughter. Turn left to the square.

The Norman church overlooks the village. Nearby is the mound (on which the castle was perched) and lovely cottages which were restored

Drive and Stroll

by the celebrated Lutyens in 1906. The Manor House is said to be the finest example of Elizabethan architecture in the Cotswolds.

⑤

Follow the road through the village. Turn left at a junction. At the next road junction turn right. The lane climbs to a T-junction. Turn left. Within ¼ mile take a wide track right. Another path (the Macmillan Way) joins our path.

⑥

Drop down to a junction of tracks by the river. Join the Windrush Way and go left. The hidden River Windrush is on the right. Follow the clear path to the A429.

⑦

Cross and turn right to a road junction and turn left by a bridge.

The bridge superseded a ford across the River Windrush. The ford was made by the 2nd Roman Legion who had their posting house here. It was the 2nd Legion army who laid out the Fosse Way.

⑧

Walk along the lane with water on the right. By a house called Speyside take a path on the right to return to the river. Bear left to cross a footbridge. Continue with the water now on the left. Go through gates. Nearing a house bear right over the pasture to a kissing gate and continue to a road. Turn left to the centre of Bourton-on-the-Water.

Places of Interest Nearby

Just south of Bourton-on-the-Water and reached by footpaths off the Rissington Road are many pools formed from old sand and gravel workings. These are now a great place not only for fishermen seeking elusive carp but also for a vast number of wildfowl who are attracted to the waters. The **Salmonsbury Meadows** are a nature reserve with notices to tell us about the interesting flora and fauna.

11 Northleach

Hampnett village: the church is Norman

The Walk 2½ miles
Map OS 1:50,000 Landranger 163 Cheltenham and Cirencester Area.
GR 109149

How to get there

Go 9 miles north-east of Cirencester along the A429. At crossroads and traffic lights in Northleach find the car park on the left by the old prison.

Drive and Stroll

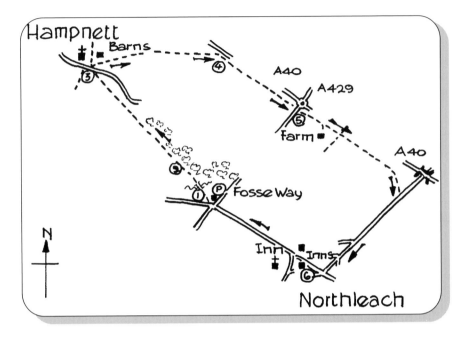

Introduction

Mercifully the town of Northleach is away from the busy main A429 but travellers are drawn to the place by the grandeur of the church tower. This dates from the 15th century when the religious fervour of the time resulted in the Perpendicular-style church.

The town belongs to the past and unlike other 'wool towns' has been content to forget its wool trade and remain a village with much that has changed little since the Middle Ages. Here are many buildings of the past – the 16th-century almshouses, timber-framed houses with overhangs, a tall gabled school building and a 17th-century manor house.

There is the old market place with its war memorial and places with wide stone archways through which the horses and woolpacks could pass into the yards behind. The church tower overlooks everything.

Northleach does have a river but it is hardly perceptible at the head of the Leach valley. 'Leach' comes from the Saxon word which means 'stream'. Around is the open rolling limestone countryside – terrain which favoured the vast numbers of sheep and which resulted in the wealth of wool merchants.

The day of the sheep has given way to the day of the grain field – that is where the money is today!

The field paths climb out of the valley to the little village of Hampnett. It is here that the River Leach has its spring and there is little else today with only the skylark to add to the peace and tranquillity but it was on a main coach-route before the coming of the turnpike roads. Hampnett has a Norman church. The track over the uplands leads to the Roman's Fosse Way and pathways go back into Northleach.

Refreshments

There are many pubs and tea rooms in Northleach. The Sherborne Arms in the Market Place is open all day every day. It is proud of its 'Award-winning chef'. Among the fine things offered are unsual fillings for baguettes including 'fresh Cornish crab and lime mayo'. There is also a daily 'Specials Board'. This place really welcomes walkers. Telephone 01451 860241.

THE WALK

①

Out of the car park turn right then right at the crossroads.

The large building (which now houses the offices for the Cotswold Area of Outstanding Natural Beauty and a countryside museum) was once a prison. It dates from 1790 and was the work of Sir George Onesiphorus Paul who devoted himself to the reform of the English penal system.

Within a few steps go through a kissing gate on the right. Take the direction indicated to go over a bridge in the far right diagonal corner. Keep the heading to walk to a stile again in the far diagonal corner of the field by a wood. Keep ahead in a meadow never far from the wood on the right – called Prison Wood. Climb a corner stile.

②

We are now in a huge arable field. Keep the old direction now heading towards a church tower. (Note: if the path is difficult and not reinstated after sowing there is a lane just to the right.) Go through a kissing gate out of the field. On the lane turn left to Hampnett.

The hilltop village has a large green with handsome houses around it. The Norman church perhaps suffered from the stencilled decorations of the 1880s. There are some fine carvings of birds on the chancel arch and a fragment of a medieval cross in the churchyard.

③

After visiting the church, retrace your steps along the lane to the entrance to Manor Farm. Here there is a signed bridleway. Go through a metal gate and walk to the right of barns. Follow the cart track over the open countryside.

Just before a gate to a main road turn right to walk alongside a left hand wood. Go through a gate to the Fosse Way.

The Fosse Way was the straight military highway which the Roman engineers laid from Lincoln to the coast in the south-west.

Cross to the opposite footpath signed along a farm drive. As the drive sweeps right to the farm keep ahead along a grassy hedged way. At the end a path crosses ours. Keep ahead along the straight bridleway with the main road just to the left. The wide track leads to a lane. Turn right. The lane goes to Northleach.

Turn right and follow the main street to the A429.

Places of Interest Nearby

The church in Northleach is well worth a visit. Among the many gems is the vaulted south porch 'as perfect as anything of its kind'. There is a magnificent stone pulpit and some renowned brasses reminding us of the wool merchants of the town. Some say these make up the finest set of brasses in England as they depict the life and manners of the merchants over two centuries.

Just off the square is the interesting museum called the **World of Mechanical Music**. It is housed in what was Woodlands Grammar School named after its wool-merchant founder. It is a living museum of various kinds of self-playing instruments. This is a place not to be missed. It is open every day from 10 am. Telephone 01451 860181.

12 Windrush

The green at Windrush

The Walk 2 miles
Map OS 1:50,000 Landranger 163 Cheltenham and Cirencester Area.
GR 193131

How to get there

From Burford where many roads (including the A40, A361 and A424) meet take the B4225 from the main street. Within half a mile go right along a lane signed to Little Barrington then continue to Windrush. Parking is available on the quiet roadside by the green near the church.

Drive and Stroll

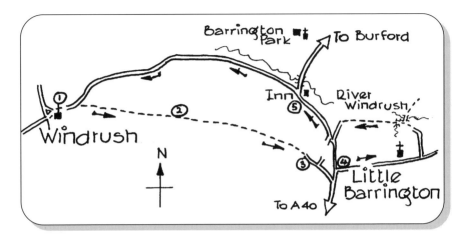

Introduction

Surely the very name of Windrush conjures up the essence of the typical idyllic English country scene. Some call this 'Wind in the Willows' landscape!

The little River Windrush meanders through a tranquil green valley and the village of Windrush is a delight. There is a triangular green guarded by a church which has stonework that reminds us that the building has been 'on duty' since the time of the Normans.

In the church dedicated to St Peter there are treasures from many ages. There is a fine roof and font, both from the 15th century, a medieval screen and a pulpit with carved roses and dragons left to us by the Jacobeans.

The route follows level fieldpaths to Little Barrington with its steep green. On the other side of the valley is the great house of Barrington Park which was built with stone from local quarries. A little lane goes by the village church with its 15th-century embattled tower.

The track drops down to the river at an old crossing place, then there is a path back to the centre of the village. On the return leg to Windrush there is a finely-sited inn which has a garden nudging the river for those sunny-day walks.

Refreshments

The Fox Inn (open all day) at Little Barrington is a noted Donnington house. Even the simple fare like soup, sandwiches and baguettes are wonderul but you will have to take your time just to digest the extensive menu of the big meals! The 'prettiest pub-setting in the Cotswolds is here' we are told! Telephone 01451 844385.

THE WALK

From the village green at Windrush walk along the lane with the church on your right.

The church has three remaining scratch dials, one with 14 rays to give a clearer indication of time. Also see the rather unusual gravestones that resemble barrels with shells decorating the ends. The design is common in the area.

Within 200 yards take a signed path through a kissing gate on the right. Follow the indicated direction along a well-worn path which goes between two old trees. Pass through a far metal gate and keep ahead near a left hand wall to a stone stile in a corner.

Stone stiles are common in the Cotswolds. They are invariably just one large flat stone stuck on end in the ground. They are diminishing in number and a few years ago the Cotswold Wardens surveyed and documented them. The word 'stile' comes from the Old English 'stigel' meaning to climb.

Maintain the heading to pass an obsolete stile then continue by a left hand hedge. Climb a rise to a corner stile by a water trough. Walk over an open field just to the right of a row of electricity posts. Over a stile keep the direction across a field.

Little Barrington

Drive and Stroll

To the right are barns that were probably tithe barns. They were used to store tithes – one tenth of the produce of farms in a parish, paid to support the church and clergy.

Over a railing stile bear right to climb a stile by the barns, and walk between them to the road.

Turn right to the village green at Little Barrington.

The village green here is unusual in that it was once a quarry from which a little rivulet ran from a spring. Humble cottages around the green were probably built from the quarried stone. However, on the hillside at Taynton were vast quarries from which stones went in the building of many famous buildings like St Paul's Cathedral, Blenheim Palace and some of the Oxford colleges.

Keep ahead at the green to the main road. Turn left then immediately right. The lane passes the church. Just beyond take a little byway left (signed as a no through road). This way drops down to the river then left to the end. Do not cross the river but keep along the track to a lane to the green again at Little Barrington. Turn right along the main road.

At a road junction (by the Fox Inn) the road divides. Take the left fork lane which goes to Windrush.

To the right of the lane is Barrington Park. The great house was built in 1736 for Earl Talbot who was Lord Chancellor during the reign of George II. The estate had been the seat of the Bray family for two hundred years until purchased by Charles Talbot. You may get a glimpse of the Palladian mansion from the lane (but there are high trees!) or from the outward leg of the walk.

Places of Interest Nearby

A little over a mile along the lane from Windrush is **Sherborne**. Much of the village is owned by the National Trust. **Lodge Park** is situated on the estate which is open for fine walks throughout the year. Lodge Park was created by John 'Crump' Dutton. He loved gambling and fun living and built the lodge in 1650 as a grandstand to observe the deer coursing. The Lodge is open from March until November. Telephone 01451 844130.

13 Chedworth

Chedworth

The Walk 3 miles
Map OS 1:50,000 Landranger 163 Cheltenham and Cirencester Area.
GR 052120

How to get there

Six miles north-westwards along the A429 take a lane signed to Chedworth on the left. There is limited parking around the green at Chedworth.

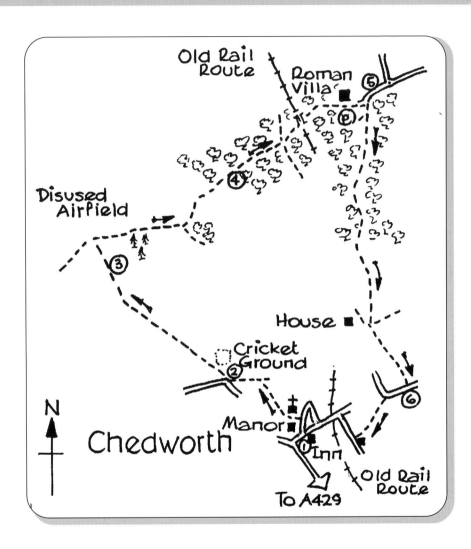

Introduction

At Chedworth is one of the finest Roman villas in the country. The walk starts at the village; it is now quite isolated but until the 1960s the place had its own railway link to Cheltenham and Cirencester. The line was on a viaduct that bisected the village before the tracks disappeared in a high green hillside below Chedworth Woods. By 1965 we read that 'the station was still boarded up with only blackbirds waiting on the platforms'.

Chedworth has a pretty little green where water gushes eternally from the bank. The scene is made complete by the inn that was built in 1610.

The route passes the manor and church before climbing the hill to a lane. Note the well-preserved milk churn on its platform that reminds us of days long past. There is a fine track alongside a beautifully-sited cricket ground.

Further along the green way a huge field is reached. The clue to its past is the terrain – the ridge-top is perfectly flat. This was an RAF airfield. There is still a blister hangar and we can see several huts left over from the war.

A delightful track through the trees of Chedworth woods follows. This passes under the rail route and drops down to the Roman villa. Do allow plenty of time to tour this fascinating site.

From the valley of the Coln we climb along the rocky track to the high hills of the beautiful Chedworth woods. We are now walking on the long-distance path of the Monarch's Way to a lane. Fieldpaths lead back to Chedworth.

Refreshments

The Seven Tuns is a 400-year-old pub that is a joy to visit. You know the sort of place – low beams, polished brass and inglenook fireplaces – plus (of course!) the warm welcome. There are a couple of dozen dishes on the bill of fare but risk the unusual rabbit terrine served with toast and red onion marmalade – different but wonderful! Then spoil yourself with a bread and butter pudding and fresh cream. Telephone 01285 720242.

THE WALK

From the little green at Chedworth walk up on the hill towards the church with the Manor House on the left.

The church dates from Norman times but the building was greatly modified in the 15th century, with windows that lightened the interior. The light shines on the Norman tub font and the pulpit where the Word has been preached since the 15th century. There is also a fine modern work from the 20th century – a sculpture of the Virgin and Child.

Take a footpath signed on the left. Go into the churchyard and along a stony path with the church on the right. At the back of the church climb steps and go through a squeeze stile to a rough hill pasture. Keep ahead alongside a right hand wall then keep climbing. At the top of the rise climb a fine stone stile.

For hundreds of years, stone stiles have been a feature of the Cotswold countryside. A huge locally-hewn flat stone made an effective barrier.

Walk along an avenue of beech trees with a vehicle way to the right. Climb another stone stile to a lane.

Drive and Stroll

The hangar at Chedworth airfield

 ②

Turn right to pass the milk churn and along a wide farm cart way. There is a cricket ground on the right. Climb a stile at the side of a gate and keep ahead to another to the old airfield.

RAF Chadworth was built in 1942 as a satellite training airfield for Spitfires. Subsequently Oxfords and Wellingtons came and went from Chedworth and for a short period the Americans were based here flying their Sentinel aircraft. The place was 'surplus to requirements' by 1950.

 ③

There is a waymark post. Follow the arrowed way over the open field to a junction of tracks. Turn right. We now walk along the old perimeter track passing a fir wood on the right. By another little wood the bridleway is signed going right. We stay on the perimeter track to pass the end of the old runway. Leave the perimeter track to walk by a right hand wire fence to woods.

④

Follow the clear track through the trees. There are many crossing ways but our path is well marked with yellow arrows. We come to a meeting of paths. Keep ahead along a way signed to 'Roman Villa'. Walk under the old railway to pass a nature reserve (Gloucestershire Wildlife Trust) to the Roman villa.

The villa was built for a wealthy Roman in the 2nd century AD and was used for 200 years until the Romans left the nearby town of Corinium (modern Cirencester). In 1864 a ferret was trapped down a rabbit warren; when men dug out the animal they unearthed traces of a mosaic and the digging has never ceased. Now there is over a mile of wall and more treasures are constantly being discovered. The villa is now in the care of the National Trust. There is a fascinating little museum on the site.

Follow the vehicle way from the villa. Within 400 yards this twists sharp left. Turn right through a gate and along a path signed as a bridleway and the Monarch's Way. As the wide way goes right keep ahead over a stile by a wooden gate. The woods are again reached. Keep along the waymarked track – a rocky path that climbs uphill. Emerging from the woods walk alongside a right hand wire fence. At a meeting of ways keep ahead to stay on the main cart track to a lane.

Turn right. Within 100 yards the lane bends right. Keep ahead through the gate. Follow the well-used track to go through another gate. At the next gate bear slightly right to pass to the right of a cottage. Go through a gate to a lane. Turn right then left at a T-junction. This returns to Chedworth village.

Places of Interest Nearby

Six miles to the south-west along the Fosse Way is the town which the Romans called Corinium but we call **Cirencester**. The museum in Park Street is a treasure-house of finds and the Roman amphitheatre on the the west side of the town can be seen.

14 Painswick

Table tombs in Painswick churchyard

The Walk 2 miles
Map OS 1:50,000 Landranger 162 Gloucester and Forest of Dean.
GR 865095

How to get there

Painswick is 5 miles south-east of Gloucester along the B4073. There is a signed car park off the A46 on the south side of Painswick.

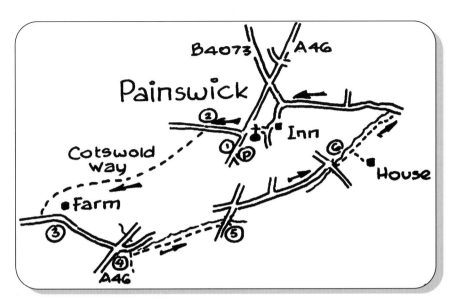

Introduction

This walk goes around the southern fringes of the charming village of Painswick, which is clustered around the most beautiful of churches although we read that bombs actually fell on Painswick in the war! The main street narrows and motorists have to steal a glance at the place of worship surrounded by table tombs and the 100 clipped yews. Actually legend says there will always be 99 – number 100 will never thrive.

But why 'Pain'? Simply that the manor was held by the lord – Pain Fitzjohn. The 'wick' shows the place was on one of the ancient salt ways that criss-crossed the kingdom.

Painswick was another place that had a vibrant industry of cloth manufacture in the 15th century. Here it would have been a cottage industry with the later processes like fulling and weaving performed in the mills – we pass several on the route. By 1608, a third of all men in the village were engaged in the wool trade.

We start the walk at the church then walk along Edge Lane. The route is through farmland to a lane. Over a main road, the lane leads to a mill – now converted to a fine mansion. We walk along a delightful path that hugs the fast-moving stream.

The final path hugs a brook before we climb out of the valley to Painswick.

Drive and Stroll

Refreshments

There are several inns in Painswick. Popular with walkers is the Royal Oak in St Mary's Street. The food is good wholesome fare with old favourites like steak and kidney pie and home-cooked ham. There is a courtyard garden for those sunny days – and the pub is happy to serve tea! Telephone 01452 813129.

THE WALK

From the car park turn right along the A46 to the church.

St Mary's church dates from the 15th century. In the Civil War the Parliamentarians took refuge here. There are still shot marks on the tower and red stones in the fabric are evidence of fire damage. The old font was destroyed so the one we see today is modern – dated 1661! Behind the church are some unusual metal stocks. The lovely slender 174 ft high spire was taken down stone by stone and exactly rebuilt after an electric storm in 1883.

Go through the lych-gate – it was built with timbers rescued after the spire fell – and cross the main road.

The house to the right is Hazelbury House which was owned by the Packer family, leading cloth manufacturers in the 17th century. The Palladian house has three storeys and was designed by the noted John Wood.

Places of Interest Nearby

Three miles to the west of Painswick is **Haresfield Beacon**. This is a most spectacular viewpoint with steep scarp edges on three sides of the promontory that protected an Iron Age fort. The name is derived from Hersa's Feld – Hersa was the Saxon who ruled this land. From here you gaze across the ribbon-like Severn to the Forest of Dean. From Painswick go along Edge Lane. At the main road go right then left along the lanes signed to the Beacon.

Three miles north of Painswick, along the A46, is **Prinknash Abbey**. The Benedictine abbey dates from 1928 and was established by monks from Caldy Island. It is famous for its distinctive pottery. The opening hours vary so phone before visiting: 01452 812455.

The attractive post office at Painswick

(2)

Walk about 200 yards down Edge Lane. Look for a path signed through a kissing gate on the left. Take the arrowed direction along the left hand side of some pasture. We are now on the Cotswold Way and the route is well waymarked through fields and by farmsteads. Eventually climb a meadow to emerge on a lane through a new metal kissing gate.

 (3)

Turn left to pass a farm. The narrow lane drops down to a main road.

 (4)

Cross to the opposite lane. Drop downhill for 100 yards. Take the signed path on the right by King's Mill

House. Go along the vehicle way. Go left through a gate and over the bridge by the mill race. The path keeps near the left hand brook to a lane.

 (5)

Proceed left to a crossroads. Turn right along King's Mill Lane.

 (6)

At a T-junction turn right. Cross the water and at once take a path through a gate (marked Mill Farm) left. Within 200 yards the vehicle way goes right to a house. We keep ahead by a left hand brook to climb a stile. Follow the well-walked path to a lane. Turn left to return to Painswick.

15 | Burford

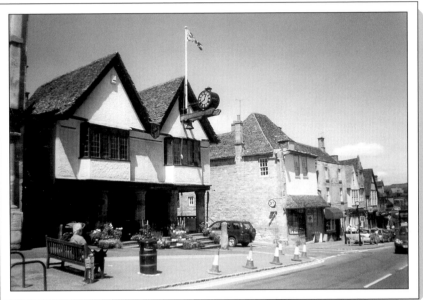

The museum in Burford

The Walk 5 miles
Map OS 1:50,000 Landranger 163 Cheltenham and Cirencester Area.
GR 253124

How to get there

Burford lies at the junction of many busy roads – the A424, A361 and the A40 – some 20 miles north-west of Oxford. There is a car park near Burford church.

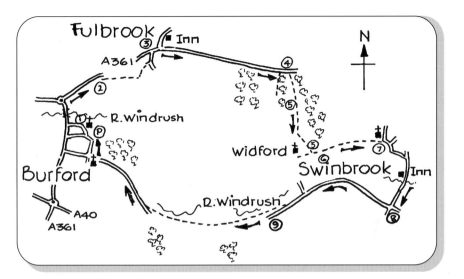

Introduction

Burford is another of those Cotswold towns whose wealth was founded on wool and, from that, we can appreciate beautiful places today. The main street rises steeply from the ancient bridge and is lined by buildings (no two the same) of mellowed stone. As one old guide book says Burford is a 'true town, with a beginning and an end . . . where, beyond the river and its bridge no houses straggle, but green fields, cows and willows come right up to the streets'.

With such beauty it is suggested you walk around the town before setting off on the route. You can see the Grammar School buildings which have been here since 1571 and the row of almshouses that were a gift to the town from Warwick the Kingmaker in 1471.

The Tolsey was the house where the wool merchants met and another fine 16th-century mansion by the River Windrush was built by Symon Wysdom, the benefactor of the Grammar School.

Overlooking the town is the church with a slender steeple. The place has fine work by the Norman masons but much is from the 15th century. Nearby is a playing field which was a bloody battleground in AD 725 when the Anglo-Saxons defeated the Mercians.

So having crossed the narrow three-arched bridge over the Windrush we soon leave the busy road and take a footpath to the village of Fulbrook. There is now a quiet lane section. A footpath dips down through woods and fields to a deserted village where the old church in a meadow has survived.

Drive and Stroll

A fine pathway through the water meadows leads to Swinbrook with a fascinating church where the Mitfords worshipped after leaving Batsford (see Moreton-in-Marsh walk, page 26). Another path on the other side of the Windrush goes back to Burford.

Refreshments

There are many inns and tea rooms in Burford but along the route is the Swan Inn at Swinbrook. It is beautifully sited by the river and sitting outside on a fine day is a delight. The range of food is wide but try their salads (in summer) or soups (on cooler days). There are also many rarer dishes. How about trying the baguettes filled with smoked bacon and melted brie or smoked salmon and cucumber? Telephone 01993 822165.

THE WALK

①

From the car park by the church walk to the main street. Turn right to drop down to the river. Cross the bridge and take the right fork at the road junction to go along the A361.

②

Within 300 yards take a path on the right signed by Cotland House. Swing left over a stile and walk along a fenced way to a field. Keep ahead at the sides of fields. At a stone stile on the left is a signed junction of paths. Over the stile, walk by the side of the field to a stone stile leading to a road. Turn left to return to the main road at Fulbrook.

The name of the village does not signify a full stream but as recorded in the Domesday Book of 1086 – Fulebrock or 'foul brook'.

③

Turn right then right again along a lane towards Swinbrook.

④

After almost a mile along the quiet lane and just past a signed bridleway on the right take a signed footpath over a stile on the right.

⑤

The path drops down Dene Bottom with woods each side to Widford.

Widford is a deserted medieval village. There are few traces on the ground but there is an interesting isolated little church in a field.

⑥

At the junction of paths after you have passed the church, there is a footpath signpost. Turn left along the way signed to Swinbrook. Go through a wide gap by a broken wall and follow the path to a stile by a gate. Aim to the right of far trees and continue by a wall to go through a little gate tucked in a corner. Follow a walled path to a gate to the graveyard of Swinbrook church.

St Mary's church is a fine building of mellowed stone. It has plenty of interesting features but many come to see the graves of the Mitford girls. The family lived in several houses in the district after leaving Batsford near Moreton-in-Marsh. Unity and Diana were ardent followers of the Nazis. The ashes of Diana (who married Sir Oswald Moseley) were recently interred here. In the church are impressive storeyed tombs of members of the Fettiplaces who were lords of the manor in Tudor and Stuart times. Note also the lovely small window made from reassembled ancient glass that was scattered when a German bomb landed by the church in 1940.

On the lane turn right to walk through the village and over the river. An inn is here – 'fabulous food' we are told – and it is!

Turn right at a crossroads and keep ahead at the next junction. Within 300 yards take a path over a stile on the right.

Follow a clear path by the Windrush to go over a stile. Keep ahead along a path that nudges the river now and then. Continue to a road and turn right to Burford. By the Baptist church turn right down Guildenford to the church and car park.

Places of Interest Nearby

Five miles south-east of Burford along the B4020 is the huge RAF station of **Brize Norton**. It is wonderful for seeing large transport and air-to-air refuelling tankers. Two miles south of Burford along the A361 is the **Cotswold Wildlife Park**. Besides the animals from around the world the Park has adventure playgrounds and restaurants. Telephone 01993 708877.

16 Bibury

The River Coln at Bibury

The Walk 4 miles
Map OS 1:50,000 Landranger 163 Cheltenham and Cirencester Area.
GR 117066.

How to get there

Bibury is on the B4425 about 12 miles north-west of Cirencester. There is parking alongside the River Coln in the main street.

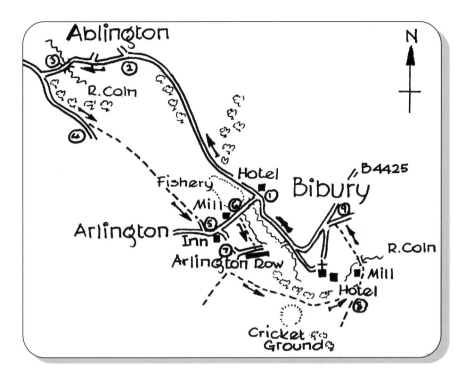

Introduction

Many villages are said to be the most beautiful village in the land. Bibury has a special endorsement to the title because William Morris said so!

I do so love one description – 'this is a place where you need not be doing anything. You can lean over the low stone wall of the village street and gaze for hours into the River Coln and watch the dappled brown shapes of trout slipping over the dappled brown gravel'. Pity about the walk!

But there are so many other things on which to gaze in this lovely place. At one end of the marshy Rack Isle where wool was once dried is the renowned Swan Hotel. The gardens (where a powerful spring adds much water to augment the Coln) are magnificent. Across the pretty bridge is Bibury Mill which houses a museum and tea room.

First we walk along some lovely lanes passing the Swan Hotel and admiring the gardens. There are then the famous trout pools from which come many of the fish that stock Cotswold rivers. The lane near the meandering river leads to Ablington – a tranquil place this, with an idyllic spot where the old bridge crosses the water.

Drive and Stroll

We climb out of the vale then take a straight footpath over the fields near the site of an ancient settlement. The path goes to Arlington.

This village (separated from Bibury by the Coln) was settled in prehistoric times and, much later, was important to the Romans along the road at their Corinium – our Cirencester.

Nearing Bibury again there is the mill and the well-walked path to the celebrated Arlington Row. These are National Trust cottages.

The route then climbs the hill and continues beside a lovely wood and a finely sited cricket ground where perhaps you can linger awhile.

Past a grand mansion is another mill where the unworked waters dance under the bridge. Across the meadow is Bibury Court; this elegant 17th-century building is now a hotel. The last part of the walk visits the ancient church that even has a stone or two carved by the Vikings. There are Saxon piers to admire and plenty of Norman work.

Refreshments

The pub on the route is the Catherine Wheel at Arlington. There is a separate 'Snacks Menu' which is comprehensive enough to satisfy all tastes. When I visited on a cool day I especially appreciated the hot baguettes – try the chicken, bacon and brie. Other folk enthused about the good value of the over-60s menu – if you qualify! Telephone 01285 740250. Snacks are also available at the Mill Museum. Telephone 01285 740199.

THE WALK

①

With the River Coln on your left, keep ahead past the Swan Hotel when the main road twists left over the old bridge.

The fine bridge has been here since the 18th century. It is a good place to spot the trout gliding under the arches.

The lane goes past the entrance to an extensive trout farm where you can try and catch your fish – then buy it! The lane goes high above the river to Ablington where there are several fine barns.

②

At a farm bear left (signed Winson). Keep ahead at a junction to pass Manor Farm which advertises bed and breakfast. Hidden over a wall on the left is Ablington Manor.

The Manor with gables and finials dates from the 16th century. It was here that a celebrated book called The Cotswold Village *was written in 1898. Its author who died when only 31 was Arthur Gibbs and the book was so popular it was reprinted ten times. He wrote with affection of his*

The mill on the River Coln

carter who had 21 children by the same wife.

 ③

Cross the Coln at a pretty spot. At a T-junction turn left along a lane signed to Barnsley. There is now a steep climb out of the valley.

 ④

Just over the brow of the hill and by a house take a signed path on the left. A fenced way ends with a stile to climb. Keep ahead to a grassy horse-gallop. Cross directly over to a sheep pasture and continue alongside a wire fence on the left. Climb two corner stiles and keep the heading over an open field. Go to the right of barns and pass through a corner stile by a wide metal gate. Cross a vehicle way and go over a stone stile. There is now a well-used path by the left hand border of a large field. By a house climb a stone stile and keep ahead through fields and along a house drive to a road.

 ⑤

Turn left to pass the inn and drop down the hill. Before the river we come to the mill on the left.

Bibury Mill was once a grain mill powered by the strong waters of the River Coln. It is listed in the Domesday Survey of 1086. The machinery still works.

Drive and Stroll

(6)

Opposite the mill take a signed path along the mill race and Rack Isle to the famous Arlington Row cottages.

The buildings were once a wool factory and the wool was laid out to dry naturally on the marshy land that is Rack Isle. All of this is now cared for by the National Trust.

(7)

Leave the cottages and walk up the hill along the lane. As the lane twists sharp right take a path signed Ready Token. Beyond some houses go through a metal gate and continue through another to a field. There is now a junction of signed paths. Take the path left along a cart track with a fence on the left. Go over a stone stile by a field gate and stay on the cart track. Pass through a corner kissing gate. Keep the heading alongside a wood to go near the cricket ground (on the right). Around a corner go through a wooden gate. Join a cart track. Pick up the side of a wood and continue to a meeting of bold tracks.

(8)

Turn left through a gate to pass near a fine house on the right. Follow the drive around bends to cross the river near a mill.

Across the grass to the left is Bibury Court which was made into a hotel. There was a house here in Henry VIII's time but the place we see today was built by Sir Robert Sackville in 1623. One wing was added 16 years later by Inigo Jones.

(9)

Continue to a road. Turn left then past a junction. At a hotel sign on the left go through a gap in the wall and join the road to the church and school. Follow the road back to the starting place.

The church of St Mary has much work of the Saxon masons. There are many memorials to the Sackville family. The font is over 700 years old and there are two rather grim brasses.

Places of Interest Nearby

About six miles along lanes to the south-east are the 'Ampney' villages along the little River Ampney. One of them is **Down Ampney** which was the birthplace of Vaughan Williams in 1872 – the son of the vicar. Perhaps his most famous hymn tune was named after his birthplace to the words 'Come down O Love divine'.

17 | Sapperton

Brunel's tunnel at Sapperton

The walk 4 miles
Map OS 1:50,000 Landranger 163 Cheltenham and Cirencester Area.
GR 948033.

How to get there

Five miles west of Cirencester along the A419, take a lane on the right
signed to Sapperton. Park on the road near Sapperton church.

Drive and Stroll

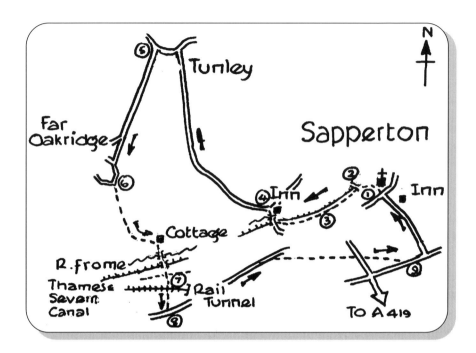

Introduction

The high Cotswolds west of Cirencester presented big problems to the railway and canal engineers. Their solution was to construct long tunnels through the soft limestone. At Sapperton (where we start the walk) the long-defunct Thames and Severn Canal enters a 3,817 yards long tunnel. The waterway was completed after five years' work in 1789 and closed in 1911.

The nearby railway tunnel is a more modest 1,855 yards long and was a Brunel masterpiece on his London to Gloucester line. The railway opened in 1845.

From Sapperton's hilltop church we drop down to woods which hide the canal tunnel entrance with its ornate castellated stonework. There is now a stroll along the track that was once the canal towing path. (There are active plans to restore the canal.)

Green and lush vegetation grows in the damp terrain. There are marsh flowers and pools where wildfowl gather. There are ferns and wild lilies, and dragonflies glint in the sunshine.

We next have a stretch of walking along attractive narrow lanes and through many woods as we climb out of the Golden Valley through hamlets like Daneway and Tunley.

The route drops into the valley and returns to the former canal at a nature reserve. At a railway crossing we can wait awhile to see an express train (once from the Great Western Railway) thundering into Brunel's tunnel.

There is a steep climb through woods to a lane. This leads to a bridleway. It is edged with trees and (being on a great estate) may well have been a mile-long ride for the gentry. Lanes lead back to the pretty village of Sapperton.

Refreshments

The Bell at Sapperton is a splendid country inn. There is even a space to park your horse! What I particularly like about this pub are the terraces and gardens where sitting out on a warm day is a joy. The menu is a little upmarket but none the worse for that! Try the crayfish salad or grilled halibut. The place is open daily for food 11 am to 2 pm and 7 pm to 9.30 pm. Telephone 01285 760298.

THE WALK

①

Go into the churchyard and keep the church on your right.

The church (approached along a yew-fringed path) was greatly rebuilt in the 18th century but the tower and spire have looked over the Golden Valley of the River Frome for 600 years. Inside the church the fine woodwork came from the Elizabethan Sapperton House when it was demolished in 1730. The font is from the 15th century.

Past the porch go through a little gate to a footpath. Turn left. Within a few steps take a vehicle way to the right. After 150 yards turn right alongside a wall to pass a cottage. Continue through a kissing gate to a hill pasture.

 ②

Take the indicated direction to drop down the steep hillside towards woods. Climb a double stile. Walk down steps to the canal tunnel entrance.

This is the start of the two mile tunnel. The canal was once described by a novelist as 'a band of silver across a valley of gold'. The waterway always suffered from a shortage of water. At first a windmill pumped water from Thames Head, four miles to the south-east. There was then a Boulton and Paul pumping engine and finally a Cornish machine until the canal was abandoned.

 ③

Cross to the towing path on the far side. Follow the line of the former canal. Go through a squeeze stile

Sapperton's church has kept watch for 600 years

then another to a lane at Daneway. Turn right. At the junction is an inn.

The Daneway Inn was originally the Bricklayer's Arms. It was a popular inn with the bargees. At the other end of the tunnel is still the Tunnel House deep in the woods at Coates.

 ④

Turn left at the junction. The lane climbs steeply then goes through beautiful beech woods. At a junction take the way left with a lovely garden and pool on the left.

Over the hill is the Slad Valley – the area immortalised by Laurie Lee in his Cider with Rosie.

⑤

At the next junction go left. When the lane divides take the left hand fork then ahead at the next meeting of ways.

 ⑥

We reach a vehicle way on the left signed to Trilis. Follow this wide, rough track to drop down to a cottage. Continue along the stony footpath going steeply downhill. At the valley floor we come to the former canal again. There is a sign to say there is a nature reserve here.

The nature reserve is administered by the Gloucestershire Wildlife Trust. It has over 70 reserves in the county covering 2,500 acres. This reserve in the Sapperton Valley contains one of the most luxuriant small wetlands in Gloucestershire.

At a crosstrack keep ahead into the woods. The line of the path is a little obscure at first but the path is soon clear climbing uphill. The woods were once important for coppicing.

Coppicing used beech or hazel trees. The shooting branches would be cut at the base and woven into sheep hurdles.

Climb through the trees to stiles at a crossing place of the railway.

Brunel's tunnel can now be seen to the left. The railway even to this

point has had a steep climb of 1 in 90 out of the valley of the River Frome.

Go over the railway to climb a metal stile. The path beyond leads to a lane.

Turn left. Within ¾ mile take a signed bridleway which lies just off the road by a pole fence on the right. Follow the straight way through a barrier to a road. Cross over to continue along the bridleway to another road.

Turn left, then left again, to Sapperton.

Places of Interest Nearby

Twelve miles to the south-west of Sapperton (and 3 miles south-west of Tetbury) on the A433 is **Westonbirt Arboretum** which has one of the finest collections of trees in Europe. Plantings were first made in the 1820s by Robert Holford. There are now 116 acres planted with rare and beautiful trees. The arboretum is open daily. By the way – on the way out of Tetbury you will pass Highgrove House, the home of Prince Charles.

18 | Dursley

Cam Long Down overlooks Dursley

The Walk 2 miles
Map OS 1:50,000 Landranger 162 Gloucester and Forest of Dean.
GR 752980

How to get there

From the A38, go south along the A4135. Dursley is reached after 3 miles. The car park is signed from the centre of Dursley. Go along May Lane to the car park opposite the inn in Hill Road.

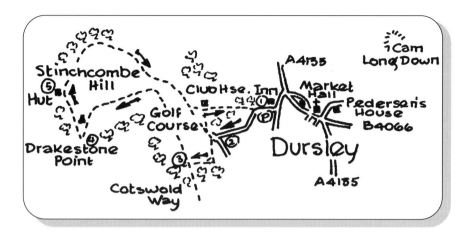

Introduction

Dursley, where this walk starts, is a town that has seen many changes in fairly recent years. Its great past was of wool. When the work of the north Cotswold towns like Chipping Campden (the sorting, grading and export of fleeces) ended, the treating and manufacture of wool cloth moved to the south of the county where there was an adequate supply of water. Many Dutch craftsmen were persuaded to come to these parts to manufacture cloth.

It is even said that some were given English surnames so that they could be assimiliated into the social structure of the region. It is thought that the Webb family were such people – they were to become the leading cloth makers of Dursley. In 1540, the chronicler Leland described the town as 'a praty clothing town, well occupied with clothiers'.

When hard times came to Dursley, the resolute folk switched to other industries. One of the most famous firms was RA Lister which was established in the mid-19th century. They were to become one of the leading companies in the world in the manufacture of diesel engines. In their early years they made cycles with distinctive gears invented by a Dane, Mikael Pedersen. We can see the house where he lived in Dursley.

After a tour of the town (with its oddly-shaped Market House at the end of the pedestrianised main street) we climb Hill Road which heads towards vast woodlands. The road narrows into a fine lane twisting away through magnificent trees.

The summit is a large plateau which is covered with a golf course. We border the grass to reach the woods and join the long-distance path of the Cotswold Way. The woods are soon left and the path continues around the periphery of the golf course.

Drive and Stroll

The steep scarp edge of the Cotswolds is reached with those magnificent views far across the Severn Vale and the Forest of Dean beyond. On clear days there are fine views of those giant suspension bridges over the river.

The return to the car park is down a rough track and through the woodlands of Stinchcombe Hill that are welcomingly cool on hot summer days.

Refreshments

There are many pubs and eating places in Dursley including a wonderful ice-cream parlour! Opposite the car park is the Old Spot Inn. In summer, this flower-bedecked inn has a choice of six real ales. The food is mainly traditional pub fare (jacket potatoes, sandwiches, ploughman's, etc) but there are one or two more intriguing dishes like chicken fajitas. Opening hours are 11 am to 3 pm and 5 pm to 11 pm but open all day at weekends. Telephone 01453 542870.

THE WALK

As the walk is short, you may like to take a brief perambulation around the town centre.

The 18th-century Market Hall is built on 12 arches. It is enhanced by a fine statue of Queen Anne. Nearby is the parish church. The chapel was built by Thomas Tanner, a wool merchant; the tower was built by Thomas Sumision in the early 18th century. Pedersen's House in Long Street is marked by a plaque.

Turn left out of the car park to walk along Hill Road. The road narrows into a country lane which climbs Stinchcombe Hill.

At a T-junction on the summit, turn right to the vast open grassy space. At once turn left along a vehicle way signed as a no-through-road.

When the vehicle way ends keep ahead along a footpath and enter woodlands. After 100 yards there is a crossing track. Turn right to the grasslands. Immediately take the path left. We are now walking along the Cotswold Way.

The Cotswold Way has been designated as a National Trail. It therefore receives generous Government funding. The 100-mile-long route follows mainly footpaths marked with the acorn logo along the top of the escarpment from Chipping Campden to Bath.

Walk at the borders of the golf course, following waymarks. Pass a car park and continue along an indistinct path for about ¾ mile. If in doubt keep to the high ground.

The viewpoint of Drakestone Point is reached.

At 700 ft, this is the highest bluff on the southern edge of the plateau with views through almost 240 degrees. Nearby is a seat on which we can read that the lands were given to the public through the generosity of Sir Stanley William Tubbs in 1930.

Retrace steps then walk to the left of the triangulation plinth. We reach a shelter.

This too was erected in memory of Sir Stanley and is a good place for eating your sandwiches when the wind blows!

Resume walking at the edge of the golf course then follow the path to again reach the car park. Walk along the tarmac vehicle drive. When near the club house on the left cut across to the building. Take the path on the right hand side of the club house. Drop down the steep hill through the woods to Hill Road. Retrace your steps to the car park.

Places of Interest Nearby

Five miles north-east along the A4135 is Slimbridge. Here follow the signs to the **Slimbridge Wildfowl Trust**. At all times of the year multitudes of birds will be seen. The place is open every day from 9.30 am to 4.30 pm. Telephone 01453 890333.

19 | Cotswold Water Park

Cotswold Water Park

The Walk 3½ miles
Map OS 1:50,000 Landranger 163 Cheltenham and Cirencester Area.
GR 060932

How to get there

From Cricklade (6 miles south-east of Cirencester) drive west on the
B4040. Within 2 miles turn right along a lane signed to Waterhay where
there is a free car park.

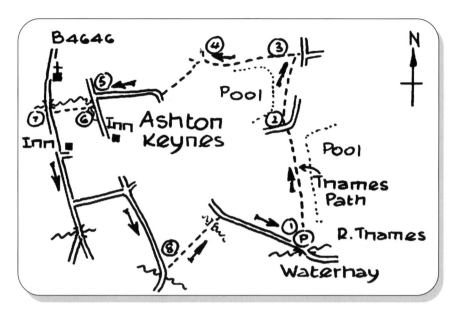

Introduction

The Cotswold Water Park covers an area of several square miles in the upper reaches of the River Thames. It is an area rich in sand and gravel deposits with many quarries still being actively worked. Some water-filled quarries have been given over to leisure activities – sailing and all sorts of boats, fishing and even man-made inland beaches.

The pools have an unusual beauty which is enhanced by many tree-lined islands. Wildfowl like the waters too, especially the graceful herons.

The countryside here is constantly changing; vast pools are drained and the land infilled. Others are drained to reveal further deposits to be extracted – deposits which were once considered too uneconomic to obtain.

This changing scenery did cause a problem in finding a pleasant walk in the park as pathways are constantly re-routed. However, east of Ashton Keynes much work has been undertaken to provide wonderful and permanent tracks by the waterside.

The starting point is off a lane by a bridge over the infant Thames. Here there is the car park and benches and tables for those summer picnics. I like the cycle rack here with the wrought-iron bikes! We follow a new track which is part of the Thames Path – a long-distance route which follows the river from its source to the capital.

There are lovely still waters each side of the track which we follow to the

Drive and Stroll

village of Ashton Keynes where there are two inns. A fine path crosses the Thames then follows the tranquil waterway to a road.

Quiet lanes go to a bridleway – a green way which goes over a brook at an idyllic ford. A final short stretch of lane-walking leads back to the car park.

Refreshments

There is one inn on the route and another just off the route at point 7. The White Hart at Ashton Keynes positively welcomes ramblers and children (smaller portions and plenty of chips). Although there is the usual pub fare the menu also offers many rather good unusual dishes. Try the brie, bacon and cranberry relish ciabatta, or the maple and thyme roasted ham with free-range eggs. The White Hart is open daily 12 noon to 2.30 pm and 6 pm to 11 pm. Telephone 01285 861247.

THE WALK

①

A bridleway starts at the far side of the car park. Go over a ground barrier by a metal gate. At a signpost keep ahead along a way signed Thames Path. Within 400 yards is another signpost. Again keep ahead along a track signed as a bridleway. Pass through a gate to a lane.

The Thames Path is a waymarked route that follows footpaths, lanes and towing paths along the valley of the river from the start a few miles from Cirencester to the end in London.

 ②

Cross to the opposite path through a gap. The path is now straight with a pool away to the left. Keep ahead to a junction of tracks. Turn left along a path signed Ashton Keynes.

 ③

Follow the well-used path through a stone stile then join a quarry road. Maintain the heading. When the quarry road bears right keep the old heading along a path.

 ④

When confronted by a hedge turn left through a kissing gate. Follow the path through another hunting gate. The path goes along the gardens by cottages to a road at Ashton Keynes. Turn right.

There are many place names which include the word Ashton in the United Kingdom. It is derived from the Old English 'aesctun' or 'the place where the ash tree grows'. The manor was held by Robert de Keynes in the 13th century. Keynes comes from Cahagnes in Normandy.

At a T-junction turn left along the road. Within 30 yards turn right by the shaft of an old cross.

In English towns and villages many crosses were built in medieval times at places where itinerant missionaries preached.

Go over the small bridge and follow the vehicle way called Church Walk beside the River Thames. Keep ahead along the footpath still with the water on your right.

The name Thames perhaps comes from a common Old English root that means 'dark river'. Others say that the word (common with other words like the Tame and Thame) may have connections with the Scandinavian 'ta' – 'fluid or water'.

At a road turn left. Go past one junction (pub along the lane to the left). At the next junction take the narrow lane left. The lane leads to a crossroads. Turn right (signed to Wootton Bassett).

Within 500 yards the lane twists sharp right. Turn left along a farm track – an unsigned bridleway. When the track goes into a field keep the old heading along a green path. At a ford go over the footbridge and continue to a lane. Turn right to the car park.

Places of Interest Nearby

Five miles along lanes north-east of Ashton Keynes is the **source of the Thames**. It can be approached across the fields from the Thames Head Inn on the A433. However be prepared to be disappointed with thoughts of the 'mighty Thames' as we see little more than a muddy depression! There are earthworks nearby showing where the Thames and Severn Canal once ran (see the Sapperton walk, page 80).

20 | Wotton-under-Edge

The magnificent tower of St Mary's church

The Walk 5 miles
Map OS 1:50,000 Landranger 162 Gloucester and Forest of Dean.
GR 758933

How to get there

From junction 14 on the M5 follow the B4509 and B4058 which are signed to Wotton-under-Edge. The car park in The Chipping is well signed in the centre of town.

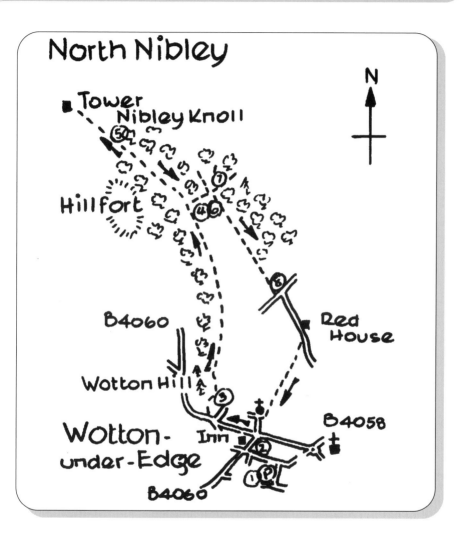

North Nibley

Introduction

This walk goes to a monument that is a landmark for many miles as it was built on a knoll high above the valley. The starting place is Wotton-under-Edge.

Wotton was in Saxon times 'wudu tun' – the farm in the wood. The 'under Edge' was added in the 14th century to accentuate its position below the Cotswold escarpment. It became an important wool town and at a census taken in 1608 half of all the workers were engaged in the wool trade. By the early 19th century the trade had drastically declined and (like Dursley) the town switched to other industries.

There is a rather dull road out of town but we soon see a path to climb to leave the traffic behind. Past a viewpoint by the Wellington plantation we are soon walking in the fine woodlands of Brackenbury Ditches. We are following the Cotswold Way so waymarking is now much improved with its designation as a National Trail.

Much of the area of the Iron Age camp is now covered with the trees of Westridge Wood but one can appreciate the large size. The floor of the woodlands is covered with bluebells in springtime which delicately scent the air.

We emerge in grasslands which are dominated by a tall tower. This is the monument to William Tyndale, the great translator of the Bible into English. It may be possible to locate the key to climb the tower but there are many puffing steps to the top where the climb is rewarded with splendid views.

We retrace our steps to the edge of woodland then walk on two sides of a large field to a lane. There are good views over the town before reaching the prominent former Tabernacle.

Refreshments

Wotton is well served with inns and cafés. There is also a pub in North Nibley but that entails dropping down a steep hill then climbing back up to the route. In Wotton the Royal Oak in Haw Street is a traditional family pub which is open all day. The menu is good basic fare with large portions for hungry walkers. Telephone 01453 842316.

THE WALK

As the car park is in the centre of Wotton it is convenient to walk around the town before tackling the route.

The car park is on The Chipping which is the old English word for 'market'. The town was all but destroyed in the reign of King John. The church of St Mary was rebuilt but much of what we see dates from the work done in 1400. There is a magnificent tower that has overlooked the town since the 14th century. In Orchard Street is a plaque to Isaac Pitman, the inventor of shorthand. The Grammar School at the bottom of Long Street was founded in 1384. Perhaps the most famous building in the town is the unspoilt Jacobean 17th-century Berkeley House.

Walk down Market Street to pass the Town Hall.

The 18th-century Town Hall was once a covered market hall. The roof was supported on the Doric columns. It was converted to the Town Hall in the 19th century.

At the High Street junction turn left. The building on the corner is Tolsey House.

Tolsey dates from the late 16th century. It has had a variety of uses. It started life as the Court House. It may then have been a prison. The building is topped with an elegant bell turret and overhanging the road is a large clock erected to celebrate the Jubilee of Queen Victoria.

At the crossroads turn right (Bear Street) then left (B4060). Keep ahead at road junctions. Look for a signed path on the right.

Go up steps to the grassy area of Wotton Hill.

There is a clump of trees on the left surrounded by railings. Trees were originally planted here in 1815 to mark Waterloo. With the end of the Crimean War the trees were felled for a celebration bonfire. The site was replanted in 1887 to mark Victoria's Jubilee.

Keep well to the right of the trees and follow the clear path into woodlands. We soon have a large field on the right.

At the end of the field there is a waymark post (acorn logo). Keep ahead following the main path through Westridge Wood. To our left (largely hidden by trees and bushes) is Brackenbury Ditches.

This is an Iron Age hillfort that covers a high promontory. The fort covers six acres in the shape of a triangle with the scarp edge of the hill on two sides and the neck heavily defensible with ditches and ramparts. It is thought the site has not been excavated.

There are many criss-crossing paths through the wood but watch carefully for Cotswold Way waymarks or yellow arrows with a white centre spot.

There is a steep climb to emerge from the trees. The path is now over the grass; make for the tall Nibley monument.

The tower was erected in 1866 as a memorial to William Tyndale, the translator of the Bible. He was born towards the end of the 15th century but just where and when is not known. He had to find refuge in Germany to work on the Bible; the New Testament was completed in 1526. He never returned to Britain.

Drive and Stroll

Retrace steps through Westridge Wood to that early acorn waymark. Here turn left so the large field is now on the right.

At a meeting of five tracks take the first track right. This wide way borders the right hand field. Through a gate keep ahead along a hedged way to a lane.

Go left then right along the lane. The lane drops sharply. Ignore other paths until about 200 yards past a red house on the left. Go through a kissing gate on the right to a field. (Seats here to rest awhile.) Take the clear path that drops downhill to go along a hedged path in the far left corner. Go through metal barriers. Follow paths and vehicle ways to emerge on a road by a former church.

This magnificent building was once the Tabernacle. (Now it stores furniture!) Wotton was once a great centre for Nonconformist worship with the Old Town Meeting House dating from 1701. The Tabernacle was founded by the Rev. Rowland Hill in the 19th century – he was in the post for fifty years. In his memory the nearby almshouses were built.

Walk past the almshouses to return to the town.

Places of Interest Nearby

Twelve miles to the south of Wotton-under-Edge is **Little Sodbury hillfort**. Unlike the hillfort on the walk, this one is not covered with woods so a good idea can be had of the extent of the fortification. It is said to be the finest in the Cotswolds with deep ditches and ramparts still in place; it covers 11 acres. Although built in the Iron Age it was well used by the Romans. The Saxons were also based here before going on to their great battle at Dyrham in AD 577.